Depression Book For Teens

CRAFTED BY SKRIUWER

Copyright © 2024 by Skriuwer.

All rights reserved. No part of this book may be used or reproduced in any form whatsoever without written permission except in the case of brief quotations in critical articles or reviews.

For more information, contact : **kontakt@skriuwer.com** (www.skriuwer.com)

TABLE OF CONTENTS

CHAPTER 1: WHAT IS DEPRESSION IN TEENS?

- Definition of teen depression and how it differs from normal sadness
- Common misconceptions and the importance of recognizing real symptoms
- Why acknowledging and learning about depression is crucial

CHAPTER 2: COMMON SIGNS AND SYMPTOMS

- Emotional and behavioral indicators that may suggest depression
- Physical manifestations often linked to a low mood
- Distinguishing typical mood swings from serious warning signals

CHAPTER 3: FACTORS THAT CONTRIBUTE TO DEPRESSION

- Biological, genetic, and environmental influences on teen depression
- How life events and stress can intensify depressive feelings
- Identifying personal risks and protective factors

CHAPTER 4: UNDERSTANDING FEELINGS AND EMOTIONS

- Differentiating thoughts from emotions for clearer self-awareness
- Why teen emotions can feel particularly intense
- Healthy ways to process and accept emotional ups and downs

CHAPTER 5: REACHING OUT FOR HELP

- Reasons why seeking support is vital, even when it feels difficult
- Approaches for talking to parents, friends, or professionals
- Available resources like hotlines, counseling, and online support

CHAPTER 6: CHANGING UNHELPFUL THOUGHT PATTERNS

- *Recognizing negative self-talk and cognitive distortions*
- *Strategies to challenge and replace harmful thought loops*
- *Using small shifts in thinking to gradually improve mood*

CHAPTER 7: BUILDING SELF-CARE HABITS

- *Everyday routines that nurture physical and mental health*
- *Importance of balanced eating, rest, and gentle activities*
- *Creating a personal toolkit for ongoing self-care*

CHAPTER 8: MANAGING STRESS IN EVERYDAY LIFE

- *Identifying common stressors—school, social, family—and their impact*
- *Practical tips for reducing daily pressure*
- *Relaxation techniques for immediate and long-term relief*

CHAPTER 9: ONLINE PRESSURES AND SOCIAL MEDIA

- *How internet use and social platforms can affect teen mental health*
- *Dealing with comparison, cyberbullying, or unrealistic online portrayals*
- *Setting healthy digital boundaries and mindful screen habits*

CHAPTER 10: HANDLING SCHOOL CHALLENGES

- *Balancing academic pressures, extracurriculars, and personal life*
- *Strategies for test anxiety, motivation, and time management*
- *Communicating with teachers or counselors when overwhelmed*

CHAPTER 11: FRIENDS AND PEER INFLUENCE

- *How friendships can support or undermine mental health*
- *Recognizing harmful peer pressure and setting boundaries*
- *Building balanced, respectful relationships*

CHAPTER 12: TALKING WITH FAMILY

- *Overcoming barriers to honest communication at home*
- *Finding the right time and approach to discuss emotional needs*
- *Navigating cultural differences and setting helpful family boundaries*

CHAPTER 13: DEALING WITH GRIEF AND SADNESS

- *Understanding grief as a response to various losses*
- *Safe ways to express and move through deep sadness*
- *Supporting friends who experience grief and recognizing when to seek help*

CHAPTER 14: RECOGNIZING SELF-HARM RISKS

- *Differences between self-harm and suicidal intent*
- *Warning signs that indicate someone may be self-harming*
- *Steps to take if you or a friend engages in self-harm thoughts or actions*

CHAPTER 15: HABITS THAT MAY WORSEN DEPRESSION

- *Common lifestyle factors and thought patterns that feed low mood*
- *Why isolation, poor sleep, and negative self-talk can deepen sadness*
- *Replacing unhelpful habits with healthier alternatives*

CHAPTER 16: SETTING REASONABLE GOALS

- How small, doable objectives can create motivation and structure
- Using SMART goals while respecting personal limits
- Staying flexible and adjusting targets as you grow

CHAPTER 17: ACTIVITIES THAT CAN BOOST MOOD

- Enjoyable and simple ideas for improving daily outlook
- Incorporating arts, nature, mindfulness, or social hobbies
- Benefits of gentle movement, volunteering, and personal expression

---

CHAPTER 18: LEARNING FROM POSITIVE EXAMPLES

- Finding inspiration in role models—real, historical, or fictional
- Adapting their coping methods to suit your unique situation
- Avoiding harmful comparisons and keeping perspective

CHAPTER 19: KEEPING UP LONG-TERM WELL-BEING

- Maintaining healthy routines and recognizing early warning signs
- Balancing school, relationships, and self-care over time
- Adjusting professional support and building a proactive lifestyle

---

CHAPTER 20: MOVING FORWARD AND STAYING STEADY

- Integrating learned strategies into everyday life
- Handling setbacks maturely and acknowledging ongoing personal growth
- Carrying hope, self-compassion, and realistic expectations into the future

Chapter 1: What Is Depression in Teens?

Teenage years can feel confusing for many people. It is a time when you might begin to notice changes in your body, your thoughts, and your feelings. Sometimes, it can be hard to make sense of these changes. You might wonder if what you are experiencing is normal or if there is something else going on. One of the challenges many teens face is depression. Depression is more than feeling down or sad for a short time. It is a condition that can affect how you see yourself, how you relate to others, and how you handle each day.

Depression is not simply the same as typical sadness. Feeling sad from time to time is normal. For example, you might feel sad after an argument with a friend or if you fail a test at school. These sad feelings often get better when things change or when you have time to rest and clear your mind. With depression, feelings of sadness, hopelessness, or emptiness can last for weeks or even months. They do not go away on their own, and they can make it hard to do everyday tasks.

Though depression is serious, it is also common among teens. Some people think that it only happens to adults, but that is not true. Teens can feel just as down or overwhelmed, even if they are young. Some teens do not realize they have depression, because it can look different for each person. Some teens might seem sad or down most of the time. Others might act angry, annoyed, or unable to find interest in anything. Some teens might try to keep their feelings hidden because they think they should act strong or not show weakness. They might fear that others will not understand what they are going through. Because of this, many teens keep their feelings to themselves, causing those sad or hopeless thoughts to stay inside.

There are many causes of depression. It is not just one thing. Sometimes, people have a family background where depression is more likely. That means that if a parent, grandparent, or other close relative has experienced depression, you might face a higher chance of having it too. This does not mean you must feel hopeless if that is the case. It just means you might want to be more careful about noticing signs and asking for help if you sense that something is wrong.

Depression can also happen due to events in life. When tough things happen—like losing a loved one, going through parents' divorce, or having problems at home—it can affect how you feel. Some teens might start to feel down when they do not have good support or a safe place to share their worries. Others might feel anxious or pressured due to strict rules or too many duties at home. Some might be facing bullying at school or online. All these events can lead to a state of sadness or hopelessness that does not go away.

Many people get confused about what depression really is. They might think someone who feels depressed is just lazy or seeking attention. They might say things like, "Snap out of it," or "You're just in a bad mood." But depression is more serious than that. When someone has depression, it is not as easy as deciding to feel happy again. The mind can get stuck in a loop of negative thinking, making it seem like nothing will ever get better. This loop can make it hard to enjoy hobbies or spend time with friends. It can even make it hard to get out of bed in the morning or focus on simple tasks.

Another important point is the difference between depression and typical teenage mood changes. During your teenage years, your hormones change quite a bit. You might notice your moods go up and down more often than before. This alone does not always mean you have depression. However, if you have many days in a row where you feel deep sadness, emptiness, or hopelessness, it might be a sign of something more than just normal teenage mood swings. If it makes you want to give up on things you once liked or if you feel you are not good enough day after day, it is wise to consider talking to a trusted person or a mental health professional.

Depression can also show up in your body, not just your thoughts. Some people lose their appetite and eat much less than usual. Others might find themselves wanting to eat a lot more. Some have trouble sleeping at night, while others feel so tired that they sleep much longer than before. Headaches, stomachaches, and other aches in the body can show up without a clear physical cause. These body signs often come hand in hand with the sad or hopeless feelings. Though you might only notice the tiredness or changes in appetite, these shifts can be part of a larger problem.

There are different types of depression. Major depressive disorder is what many people think of when they hear the word "depression." In this type, the sadness or emptiness lasts most of the day, nearly every day, for at least two weeks. Dysthymia, also known as persistent depressive disorder, is less intense but lasts for a longer period—sometimes for years. There is also something called seasonal affective disorder, which happens when a person feels more depressed during certain seasons, often winter when there is less sunlight. For teens, it might take time to figure out which type fits their situation. A doctor or mental health specialist can help you figure out what is going on and why it is happening.

Being aware of depression in teens is important because it can affect many parts of life. It can hurt your grades if you cannot focus at school. It can affect your friendships if you do not have the energy to hang out or talk. It can make family time stressful if you are always feeling angry or down. Sometimes, feelings of depression can get so bad that a teen might think about harming themselves or not wanting to live anymore. This is a very serious situation. If you or someone you know has these thoughts, it is important to ask for help right away. Depression can be treated, but it must be noticed first.

One challenge is that people often do not want to talk about mental health issues. They might be scared of how others will react. They might worry about being judged or laughed at. But depression is not something to ignore. If you had a broken leg, you would not try to hide it and hope it goes away on its own. You would see a doctor. In the same way, if your mind feels "broken" or stuck in a painful place, you deserve care too. There is nothing wrong with seeking help for depression or any other mental health concern.

Understanding depression is the first step in handling it. By knowing that it is a real condition that affects your brain and your thoughts, you can start to see that it is not your fault. You are not "weak" or "bad" because you feel down or empty for a long time. You are someone who needs support, understanding, and practical steps to feel better. Depression can happen to anyone. It does not choose based on how smart, strong, or popular you are. Even people who look happy on the outside could be struggling on the inside.

It might help to know that you are not alone. Many teens across the world face depression or other mental health issues. If you are feeling alone, it might be because you do not hear others talk about it. But once you find a space where people feel safe enough to open up, you realize many are going through similar issues. Talking about depression with a trusted adult, teacher, counselor, or friend can help break the sense of being all by yourself.

In fact, admitting you need help shows bravery. It is not easy to open up about things like hopelessness or sad thoughts. But seeking help means you are willing to find a way to feel better. It also helps you avoid harmful ways of coping, such as using drugs or alcohol to numb your sadness. Some teens may feel like doing things that give them a short sense of relief. But those ways do not fix the deeper problem. They can even make things worse in the long term. Learning about depression and how to handle it can help you find healthier ways to feel more stable and safe.

The good news is that depression does not have to last forever. There are many ways to treat it, including talking therapies, medicine, and changes to habits. Therapists, counselors, and doctors can guide you, but you also play a role in getting better. Learning about what depression is and how it works can give you more power over it. Once you understand that it is not just "in your head" but rather a real condition with real effects, you might feel better about speaking up and seeking help.

In the chapters ahead, we will explore many parts of depression. For now, remember that it is okay to ask questions if you think you might have depression. It is okay to talk to someone and say, "I feel sad all the time, and I'm not sure why." It is okay to share what you are going through. Depression can feel scary because it can make you think that nothing will ever improve. That is a false idea that depression creates. Things can get better when you reach out, learn more, and take steps to handle your feelings.

You might worry that people will not believe you if you say you might have depression. Sometimes, friends or family might say, "You're just a teenager. You'll get over it." But only you know how you truly feel inside. It might help to talk to a school counselor or a mental health professional who is trained to understand these concerns. They will not tell you that it is all in your head. Instead, they can help you figure out what is happening and offer you ways to find relief.

Depression can sometimes make you think about your worth as a person. You might feel worthless, as though you do not matter. But these thoughts are not true. They are a sign that you need help. You deserve to feel peace in your mind and heart, just like anyone else. If you ever catch yourself thinking, "I am useless," understand that this is part of the depression. It is not a true statement about who you are. Depression changes the way you see yourself and the world around you. It removes hope and makes the future look dark, even if it is not.

You might also feel worried about the future. If you cannot see a bright future for yourself, you might feel that there is no reason to try. These thoughts are also a common part of depression. They make the future seem bleak, and they can make a person think, "Why bother?" But teens who seek help often find that once they get the right support, their thoughts change. Suddenly, the same teen who felt hopeless last month might find pleasure in small things again. They might laugh with friends, do better in school, and see that life can be worth living.

We are all different, so depression can look different in each of us. One teen might be very withdrawn, avoiding activities and staying in their room all day. Another might keep going out but feel empty or numb. Another might act rebellious or angry a lot of the time. Despite these differences, the common thread is a sense of sadness, emptiness, or low mood that does not go away. You might also have trouble focusing on tasks and a loss of interest in activities you once found fun.

Some people might ask, "Why do teens get depressed at all? You're young, you have a whole life ahead of you. Isn't that enough to keep you happy?" This kind of question can make you feel guilty, as if you have no right to feel sad. But depression does not work that way. It is not a choice. You cannot just will it away by thinking, "I should be happy." Many things can contribute to depression, such as genetics, stressful situations, past trauma, and even natural changes in the brain during teen years. So if you feel depressed, remember it is not your fault and not a simple matter of being ungrateful or lazy.

In the following chapters, you will learn more about how to recognize signs and symptoms of depression, where to look for support, and how to handle the thoughts that come along with it. There will also be chapters on stress management and handling problems with friends and at school. But for now, keep in mind that depression is a real health condition. It is not about weakness or not trying hard enough. If you or someone you know shows signs of prolonged sadness, hopelessness, or changes in mood or behavior, it is important to take it seriously. You do not have to face it alone.

One more thing to know is that the word "depression" sometimes gets thrown around casually in everyday talk. People might say, "I'm depressed" if they are having a bad day or if something small goes wrong. This can make it confusing to figure out what real depression is. But there is a difference between feeling briefly unhappy and feeling stuck in a dark mood for a long time. Real depression is strong enough to interfere with daily life. It does not just go away when things start to look up again. Instead, it tends to stick around, affecting your self-esteem, your energy, and your hope.

Understanding the basics of depression is key to recognizing when you might need help. If you find it hard to see any good in yourself or in your future, that is a sign you should talk to a trusted person. If you feel like not getting out of bed most mornings, that is also a sign of something deeper going on. If it lasts for days, weeks, or months, it is worth seeking help. You might think you can handle it by yourself, but depression can be tricky. It can make you think you should not bother others with your problems or that they will not care. In fact, many people will care and want to help if you let them in.

Sometimes, people hesitate to reach out for help because they fear the word "therapy" or "counseling." They might think it is only for people with major problems. But therapy is simply a safe place to share your thoughts and feelings with someone who has been trained to listen and guide. They can help you figure out why you feel the way you do and how to change harmful thought patterns. The same goes for speaking with a doctor or psychiatrist who can tell you if medication might help. These are just tools that some people use to feel better, much like wearing glasses if your eyesight is poor or taking medicine for asthma.

It is also helpful to know that friends can be a source of support, but they are not always equipped to handle serious depression on their own. You might talk with friends who understand, but if you feel overwhelmed, it might be best to also seek professional help. Friends can encourage you, but they do not have all the training that a counselor or doctor has. You can still keep your friends involved by letting them know you are seeking help and might need patience or understanding from them.

If you do not have any close friends or trusted family members, consider talking to a teacher or school counselor. They are often prepared to help students who feel down or stressed. School counselors can connect you with resources, suggest support groups, or help you come up with ways to deal with tough thoughts. Reaching out to a counselor does not make you strange. It is simply a step toward feeling better.

Depression can feel like a weight on your shoulders. It can color everything in your life with a sense of gloom. But that weight can be lifted once you take the first step of understanding what you are facing and telling someone you trust. This book exists to let you know that there are answers and that you are not alone. You might not always feel ready to talk, and that is okay. But know that there is no shame in feeling depressed or in telling others about it. Getting help sooner rather than later can stop depression from getting worse. It can help you find better days and moments of ease.

In summary, depression in teens is a condition that goes beyond normal sadness. It lasts longer and can affect every part of your life, from how you see yourself to how you interact with others. Depression can stem from genetic factors, stressful events, or changes in your brain. It is common but serious, and it does not mean you are weak or flawed. Depression also does not have a single face; it can appear differently for each person. The first step is learning what it is and how it works. Once you have this knowledge, you can take action, speak up, and begin to look for help. Even if depression tries to convince you otherwise, remember there is hope and there are ways to feel better with the right support.

Chapter 2: Common Signs and Symptoms

In this chapter, we will look closely at the different signs and symptoms that can show up when a teen is dealing with depression. Although feeling sad is a common sign, there are many other ways depression can affect a person. By learning about these signs, you can recognize when you or someone you know might need help. Remember that each person is unique, and not everyone will have the same signs. Some might experience many of them, while others may only notice one or two. The important thing is to understand that these signs can be connected to depression and that they are worth paying attention to.

Feeling Sad or Down Most of the Time
Perhaps the most well-known sign of depression is a deep, ongoing sadness. This can feel like a heavy weight in your chest or a constant sense that you have no energy. You might cry easily or feel tears welling up for no obvious reason. Small problems that would not have bothered you much before might now cause you great sorrow. If you notice that you wake up most days feeling sad and go to bed feeling the same way, that can be a warning sign. This sadness does not always show on your face, so others might not realize what you are going through.

Loss of Interest in Activities
People with depression often lose interest in things they once found fun or meaningful. Maybe you used to enjoy playing soccer, drawing, or chatting with friends, and now these things feel dull or pointless. You might force yourself to go through the motions, but you do not feel the same excitement you used to. This loss of interest can make life seem boring or empty. It can also make you isolate yourself, because you no longer see the point in hanging out with others or trying new things.

Feeling Hopeless or Helpless
Depression can fill your mind with negative thoughts about the future. You might feel like nothing good will ever happen, or that you cannot change your situation. This sense of hopelessness can make you want to give up on your goals, because you believe there is no use trying. It can also lead to a sense of helplessness—like you cannot fix any of your problems, no matter what you do. These thoughts can become so strong that they take over your mind, making it hard to see any good possibilities ahead.

Changes in Appetite or Weight

For some teens, depression can cause a loss of appetite. They might skip meals or forget to eat because they have no interest in food. Over time, this can lead to weight loss and a lack of energy. For others, depression can cause an increase in appetite. They might eat more to distract themselves from sad or anxious feelings. This can lead to weight gain and guilty thoughts about overeating. Both changes can be warning signs that something deeper is wrong, especially if they last for a few weeks or more.

Sleep Problems

Depression can affect how well and how long you sleep. Some teens with depression have insomnia, which is trouble falling or staying asleep. They might lie awake for hours, thinking about their worries or feeling restless. Others might sleep far more than usual, struggling to get out of bed in the morning. They might feel tired all day, only to return to bed as soon as they can. Whether it is too little or too much sleep, this change in sleep patterns can have a negative impact on your mood and daily life.

Difficulty Concentrating

If you have noticed that you cannot focus on homework or even a simple task like reading a short article, it could be a sign of depression. When you are depressed, your mind can feel foggy or slow. You might read the same page several times and still not remember what it said. Or you might find yourself daydreaming during class, unable to pay attention to the teacher. This can cause your grades to go down, which might make you feel even worse about yourself. Difficulty concentrating can also make everyday tasks like chores feel more challenging.

Irritability or Anger

Not everyone with depression seems sad. Some teens may appear irritable, impatient, or easily annoyed. They might snap at friends or family over small issues. They might slam doors or get into arguments more often. This does not happen because they want to be mean; it is because depression can create a lot of tension and frustration inside. Anger can sometimes be a way to cope with feelings of sadness or worthlessness. If you notice that your temper is shorter than usual, and this goes on for more than a week or two, it might be a sign of depression.

Feelings of Guilt or Worthlessness
Depression can lead to very harsh self-talk. You might blame yourself for things that are not your fault. You could feel guilty about a mistake you made a long time ago, or even about things that have nothing to do with you. You might constantly compare yourself to others and conclude that you are not good enough. These feelings of guilt and worthlessness can make it hard to do anything productive, because you might feel you do not deserve good things or do not have what it takes to succeed.

Loss of Energy and Motivation
With depression, you might feel exhausted even when you have not done anything physically demanding. It might feel like you are dragging yourself through the day. Simple tasks, like brushing your teeth or taking a shower, can feel like running a marathon. This lack of energy can also make you want to skip social events or sports, because you just cannot find the motivation to go out. You might also have trouble getting your homework done, not because you do not care, but because it seems too hard to focus and push yourself.

Unexplained Physical Aches and Pains
Depression can sometimes show up in physical ways. You might have headaches, stomachaches, or other aches that do not seem to have a clear reason. You might visit a doctor and be told that nothing is wrong physically. But the pain feels real to you. This can be frustrating, because it seems like you should be able to find a cause. In many cases, emotional stress from depression can come out as physical pain. If these aches do not go away and you also have other signs of depression, it might be worth asking about whether your mood is affecting your body.

Withdrawing from Friends and Family
Teens with depression often feel like hiding away from the world. You might stop responding to texts or avoid social events. You could spend a lot of time alone in your room. This can happen because you do not have the energy or interest to hang out with people. Or you might feel ashamed and not want others to see that you are down. Some people think nobody would understand how they feel, so they stop trying to reach out. Over time, this can lead to a lonely cycle where you isolate yourself and then feel even more sad and empty.

Risky or Reckless Behavior
In some cases, depressed teens might act in ways that seem reckless. They might seek out dangerous situations or use substances like drugs or alcohol to escape

their feelings. They might drive too fast, skip school, or mix with the wrong crowd. This can happen because they feel numb and are trying to feel something, anything, even if it is risky. Or it might be a way to block out the pain they feel inside. Though these behaviors might give a short sense of relief, they often create more trouble and do not solve the root issue.

Self-Harm Thoughts or Actions
One of the most serious signs of depression is thinking about harming yourself. This can include cutting, burning, or other forms of self-injury. Some teens do this to try to release deep feelings of pain or anger, while others do it because they feel numb and want to feel something physical. Another serious concern is thinking that life is not worth living. If you or someone you know is thinking about ending their life, it is very important to reach out for help right away. Talk to a trusted adult, counselor, or doctor. This is an urgent matter and should not be ignored.

Changes in Grades or School Performance
Depression can make it tough to keep up with schoolwork. You might find it hard to focus on assignments, or you might lack the energy to do your homework. You might skip classes more often because you cannot face the day. Your grades could drop, even though you used to do well. Teachers might notice that you are not participating in class as much as before. Changes in school performance can be an important sign that you need help.

Frequent Feelings of Stress or Anxiety
While depression is not the same as anxiety, many teens experience both at the same time. You might feel on edge, worried about things like tests, friendships, or the future. You could have panic attacks where your heart races, you sweat, or you feel dizzy. Depression and anxiety can feed into each other, creating a cycle of worry, sadness, and lack of motivation. If you notice you spend a lot of time feeling tense or scared, it might be linked to depression or another mood issue.

Restlessness or Agitation
Some teens feel a sense of restlessness inside. They might tap their feet, shift in their seat, or feel like they cannot relax. They could pace around the room or feel an urge to get away from wherever they are. This restlessness can be a sign that your mind is not at ease. It might be connected to the irritability or anxiety often seen in depressed teens. If you find it impossible to sit still and calm your

thoughts, it could be worth looking into whether depression or another concern is behind it.

No Longer Looking Forward to Things
For many people, looking forward to a weekend event, a holiday, or a friend's birthday is normal. But when you are depressed, these things may not excite you at all. You might think, "Why bother? It won't be any fun." This lack of expectation or positive outlook can take away the little joys in life. Over time, you might forget what it even felt like to be eager about something. This sign goes hand in hand with feeling hopeless, which is why it is important to recognize it early.

Sudden Changes in Behavior or Personality
If you or someone you know goes from being outgoing and chatty to quiet and distant, or from being cheerful to angry most of the time, it can be a red flag. Sudden changes can happen for many reasons, but if they last for more than a couple of weeks and come with other signs of depression, it might be wise to pay attention. Changes can include things like dressing differently, not caring about personal hygiene, or neglecting things that used to matter. These shifts can reflect deeper emotional pain.

Feeling Overly Sensitive to Rejection or Criticism
Teens with depression might feel especially hurt by even mild criticism. If a teacher corrects them or a friend teases them, they might feel more wounded than usual. They could worry excessively about what others think of them, seeing every small comment as a sign of rejection. This could lead to avoiding social situations or school activities to avoid any chance of failure. Over time, they might give up on trying new things because they are so afraid of feeling embarrassed or unwanted.

Struggling to Feel Positive Emotions
Some teens describe depression as feeling "numb." They cannot feel sadness in a typical way, but they also cannot feel happiness. Everything seems flat or gray, like the emotions have been turned down to a very low level. This numbness can be scary, because it might make you think you will never feel normal again. But with the right help, many people do regain their ability to feel a full range of emotions.

How to Use This List

These signs and symptoms are not meant to scare you but to help you notice patterns. If you see several of these signs in yourself or a friend, it may be wise to speak to someone. A single sign by itself does not always mean a person has depression. For example, you might feel sad for a few days due to a breakup. That might pass without any lasting problems. But if these feelings or behaviors go on for two weeks or more and start to affect everyday life, it is time to reach out for help.

Why Teens Might Overlook Symptoms

Many teens might not realize they are depressed because they think their feelings are just "how life is." They might say, "Everyone feels this way," or, "I guess I'm just being dramatic." But real depression is not the same as normal ups and downs. If you sense that something is seriously off, trust that instinct. Talking to a professional or a trusted adult can help you sort out whether you are experiencing depression or another issue.

Sometimes, teens try to act as if nothing is wrong because they do not want to seem "weak" or emotional. They might also worry about letting their parents down. They do not want to add more stress to family members who might already have their own problems. But keeping it inside does not make it go away. In fact, it can grow bigger and heavier the longer you hide it. There is no shame in talking about your mental health. Think of it as being honest about something important going on in your life.

Reactions from Others

If you notice these signs in a friend, you might be worried about how to help. One thing to do is to gently encourage them to talk about what they are experiencing. Let them know you care and that you believe their feelings are real. You can also suggest that they talk to a school counselor or another trusted adult. If they refuse to seek help and you feel they are in real danger (for example, they talk about hurting themselves), it is important to let someone in authority know right away. Even if they get upset, it is better to be safe.

If someone in your family notices these signs in you, try not to panic or shut down. Understand that they might be worried and want to help. They might not know the perfect words to say, but if they are trying to support you, that is a good thing. You can let them know if you do not feel ready to talk yet, but also remember that ignoring the problem can make it worse.

When to Seek Immediate Help

If you or a friend has thoughts of harming themselves or feels like life is not worth living, do not wait. Speak to a trusted adult, call a helpline, or go to the emergency department. These thoughts can come on strong when someone is very depressed, but they do not have to end in tragedy. There are trained professionals who can help you get through the crisis and find a plan for treatment.

Looking Ahead

Knowing the common signs and symptoms of depression is the first step in dealing with it. If you have recognized some of these signs in yourself, do not lose heart. Awareness can help you decide to take action. This might include talking to someone about how you feel, seeking counseling, or changing some of your daily habits to better support your mental health.

In the coming chapters, we will talk more about why depression happens and how to reach out for help. We will also look at ways to handle unhelpful thoughts, manage stress, and deal with challenges at home and in school. For now, the key is to keep an open mind. If you think you might be depressed, remind yourself that you are not alone and that depression is treatable. Knowing the signs and symptoms can help you and others take these feelings seriously and get the right kind of help. You deserve support, understanding, and care. Feeling better might take time, but it is possible with the right steps and consistent effort.

Chapter 3: Factors That Contribute to Depression

Teen depression does not come from one simple cause. Instead, it can arise from many factors that overlap. These factors may be different for each person, and sometimes they come together in ways that make it more likely for a teen to experience deep sadness or other signs of depression. Understanding the factors that lead to depression can help you see that it is not your fault if you are struggling. It can also help you know what to look out for if you suspect you or someone else might be at risk.

Below, we will look at key factors that often play a role in teen depression. This chapter focuses on outside influences, personal traits, and life events that can shape how someone feels. By recognizing these factors, you can be more aware of your mood and reach out for help sooner if needed.

---

1. Family Background and Genetics

One of the strongest influences on whether a teen might get depressed is family background, sometimes called genetics. If a parent, grandparent, or sibling has experienced depression, there is a higher chance that you could experience it too. This does not mean you are certain to become depressed. It only means there is a tendency that might make you more sensitive to certain triggers.

Genetics can affect how your brain responds to stress, how quickly you recover from sad events, and how your body balances certain chemicals. This does not make anyone doomed to feel depressed forever. But it can be helpful to know that a family history of depression can raise your chances. If you realize that mental health concerns run in your family, you might want to pay close attention to your own feelings and behaviors. Checking in with a counselor or doctor early can help if you sense that you are feeling lower than usual.

---

2. Brain Chemistry

Your brain is constantly sending signals through chemicals. These chemicals help control mood, motivation, and even your appetite and sleep patterns. When you are healthy, these chemicals usually keep your mind balanced. But sometimes, a person's brain does not produce, send, or take in these chemicals in a balanced way. This imbalance can contribute to depression.

It is not always clear why brain chemistry becomes imbalanced. It could be tied to stress, lack of sleep, certain medical conditions, or genetics. While you cannot see what is going on in your brain chemistry, you can notice the effects through shifts in your mood, thoughts, and overall energy. If depression is linked to these chemical problems, it might be helped by professional support, including therapy or, in some cases, medication. But remember, only a qualified doctor or mental health professional can tell you if medication might be right for you.

3. Stressful Home Environment

Home should feel like a place where you can relax, talk about your feelings, and feel safe. But not everyone's home life is peaceful. Some teens live in households where there is constant conflict, yelling, or neglect. Others might see fighting or experience harsh discipline. These situations can increase stress and anxiety, making it harder for a young person to trust or feel secure.

When you do not feel safe or supported at home, your mind might remain on high alert, expecting more trouble at any moment. Over time, this constant worry can lead to depression. A teen in a stressful home environment might develop low self-esteem or feel helpless, because they cannot control what is happening around them. They might withdraw to their room or keep their troubles hidden, afraid to share or ask for help.

In these cases, it can be helpful to reach out to a trusted teacher, school counselor, or another adult relative. Some communities also have hotlines or youth centers. Even if your home environment remains stressful, having some safe support elsewhere can reduce the impact of ongoing conflict.

4. Bullying and Social Pressures

Bullying is a major cause of stress for many teens. Whether it happens at school or online, being teased, threatened, or isolated can damage a person's sense of self-worth. It can make you feel like you are not good enough or like you do not fit in. Some teens blame themselves for being targeted, wondering what they did wrong. But bullying is never the victim's fault.

Social pressures can also cause a sense of isolation or inferiority. You might feel that everyone else is smarter, better-looking, or more popular. You might compare yourself to classmates who always seem happy or who have many friends. This comparison can lower your mood. In the past, social pressures ended when you went home. Now, with online platforms, those pressures can continue around the clock. Seeing others post pictures or share stories about their lives may make you feel like your own life is lacking in some way.

All these social factors can build up and push a teen toward sadness or hopelessness. If this is happening, it might help to step back from the social circle that causes you stress, if that is an option. You can also talk to a counselor or a friend you trust. Recognizing how social pressures influence your mood is the first step in making changes to protect your emotional health.

5. Academic Challenges

School can feel overwhelming at times. You might have many tests, projects, and homework assignments, plus chores or responsibilities at home. If you also face pressure to get certain grades or get into a certain college, it can make you feel like you are always being judged. Some teens find that they cannot keep up, which can lead to frustration and a loss of confidence. Others might do well in school but still feel trapped by the constant drive for success.

Academic stress can feed feelings of depression if you do not have time to rest or do activities you enjoy. You might start to think you are a failure if you cannot meet your own expectations or those of your parents. Fearing failure can make you avoid studying or procrastinate, which then leads to more stress when deadlines come up. Breaking this cycle can be tough, especially if you feel alone in your worries.

One way to handle this pressure is to talk to a teacher or counselor about how you feel. They might offer suggestions on time management or help you create a less hectic schedule. Even small steps, like taking short breaks during homework time, can lower stress and help protect against depression.

6. Major Life Changes

Any big change can bring emotional difficulties, even if it is something that looks positive on the surface. These changes can include moving to a new town, switching schools, or your parents getting divorced. They can also involve gaining a new family member, such as a step-sibling, or dealing with a serious illness in the family. Sometimes, changes are simply too much for a teen to handle all at once. Feeling uncertain about the future can add to this burden.

When a major life change hits, you might feel unsteady. Your daily routines might get thrown off, and you might not know how to cope with your new reality. If you feel unsupported during these changes, you could develop symptoms of depression. You might try to hide your troubles or pretend you are okay, but inside, the stress can build.

It is wise to share your concerns with someone who can understand or at least offer a listening ear. It could be a counselor, a mentor, or a family friend. Talking about what is different and how it makes you feel can help you process the change. Even if the change cannot be undone, having someone there to support you can keep sadness or hopelessness from growing.

---

7. Past Trauma or Abuse

Experiencing a traumatic event can change how you view the world. Trauma might include physical, emotional, or verbal abuse. It might also involve witnessing violence or being in a serious accident. Trauma creates a lasting impact because it can cause you to see life as unsafe. You might develop fear or mistrust that stays, even when the danger is gone.

Teens who have gone through abuse often blame themselves or feel shame, even though it was never their fault. They might think, "I must have done something to deserve this." Over time, this self-blame can lead to strong feelings of worthlessness or ongoing sadness. It can also be terrifying to talk about the abuse, especially if the abuser is someone in the family.

If you have been through trauma, understanding that you are not at fault is critical. You deserve support from professionals who know how to help you heal. A counselor or therapist can help you work through the difficult memories and feelings. Sometimes, it takes more than one person to truly help, such as a doctor, social worker, or mental health specialist. Healing from trauma is possible, and knowing it can lead to depression is the first step in seeking care.

8. Personality Traits

Not everyone reacts to challenges in the same way. Some teens are more sensitive, anxious, or self-critical than others. While these traits are not automatically bad, they can make a person more open to feeling hurt or overwhelmed by life's ups and downs. For instance, if you tend to set very high standards for yourself, you might get stuck in negative thoughts if you do not meet those standards. Or if you are very shy, you might find it harder to ask for help or support when you need it.

On the flip side, certain personality traits might serve as protective factors. For instance, some people are naturally calm or able to see humor in stressful situations. However, if you do notice that your own traits make you prone to strong reactions or deep sadness, you can learn coping strategies. Identifying your personal tendencies does not mean labeling yourself as flawed—it means knowing where you might need extra care or guidance.

9. Hormonal and Physical Changes

Teen years bring many physical changes. Hormones rise and fall, bodies grow, and brains develop. These changes can cause mood swings and heightened emotions. Sometimes, it is hard to tell if your mood is normal or if it signals something bigger, like depression. If your body's changes are making you feel off-balance all the time, it can push you toward sadness or anxiety.

Sleep is also crucial here. Teens often have different sleep needs than younger kids or adults. If your schedule makes it hard to get enough rest, that can add to emotional difficulties. Ongoing lack of proper sleep can make it easier for stress to build up, which can lead to depression over time. Paying attention to basic self-care—like sleep, nutrition, and exercise—can help maintain a steady mood.

10. Use of Certain Substances

Some teens experiment with alcohol or drugs to try to lift their mood or forget their troubles. However, these substances can have the opposite effect in the long run. While a person might feel temporary relief, the crash afterward can deepen sadness or anxiety. Substance use can also affect brain chemistry, making it more likely that depression symptoms will appear or worsen. In addition, if a teen becomes dependent on these substances, they might lose friendships, face school problems, and feel even more isolated.

If you feel drawn to using a substance to handle your pain, it is worth seeking help before the habit grows. A counselor or support group can help you cope in healthier ways. Sometimes, teens hide their substance use because they are scared of getting in trouble. But talking honestly about it with a trusted adult can be the first step to preventing deeper harm.

---

11. Lack of Strong Support Systems

Support systems are the people and places that give you comfort, understanding, and practical help. This might be your parents, siblings, extended family, friends, teachers, coaches, or counselors. If you do not have a strong support system, you might feel alone when facing problems. You could worry that nobody cares or that nobody will help if you speak up.

Not everyone is lucky enough to have a stable family. Some might have few friends or live in a community where mental health concerns are ignored or not taken seriously. In these circumstances, it becomes even more important to reach out to any available resources, such as a school counselor or a helpline. Finding just one supportive person can make a huge difference. Feeling cared about can lower the stress that leads to depression.

---

12. Unrealistic Expectations

Whether they come from your parents, your peers, or yourself, unrealistic expectations can create intense pressure. You might feel like you have to achieve perfect grades or always be cheerful. You might think you must look a certain way or excel in every activity. These expectations can be impossible to meet and set you up for failure. When you do not meet them, you might feel worthless or guilty, which can feed depression.

The constant chase for perfection or external approval can steal your sense of joy. You might become so focused on avoiding mistakes that you lose sight of what truly makes you happy or fulfilled. If these expectations are coming from family members, it can feel like you have no way out. In such a case, talking openly with a trusted person about how the expectations make you feel could be a start toward relief. Remember that being human involves making mistakes and learning from them.

13. Chronic Physical Illness or Pain

Teens who have ongoing health problems, such as diabetes, asthma, or other chronic conditions, may be at risk of depression. Dealing with regular medical appointments, physical pain, or medication side effects can be draining. It might also affect your ability to take part in sports or social events. Watching others do things freely can make you feel left out or resentful.

This sense of missing out can wear on your mental health over time. A teen with a chronic illness might also worry about the future and whether their condition will get worse. This worry, combined with the everyday challenges of managing an illness, can make sadness or stress intensify.

If you face these issues, it can help to link up with a support group for teens with the same illness. Even if you cannot find a group in your area, online communities might exist. Knowing you are not alone in managing your health can make a difference. You can also speak to a mental health professional who has experience supporting people with chronic illness.

14. Cultural or Community Factors

Sometimes, cultural or community factors can shape how teens view themselves or how they handle emotions. For instance, if you come from a background where talking about personal problems is not encouraged, you might keep your troubles to yourself. Or you might fear judgment from relatives or community members if you admit to feeling depressed. This can stop you from seeking help early.

Teens who belong to marginalized or minority groups may also face extra stress. They might deal with discrimination, hateful comments, or unfair treatment. Feeling singled out for aspects of their identity—such as race, religion, or orientation—can lead to loneliness or anger. Over time, these feelings can develop into depression if there is no safe outlet. If you find yourself in this position, consider seeking support from community organizations or online networks that welcome people in your situation. Feeling validated and accepted is crucial.

---

15. Pressure to Fit In

Fitting in can be a big concern for teens. Sometimes, that pressure to belong can lead you to change your behavior or preferences so others will accept you. You might try to dress a certain way, like certain music, or follow trends you do not actually enjoy. If you feel forced to hide your true self, it can build negative emotions like shame and sadness.

This pressure can come from peers, media, or even your own mind. You might think, "If I do not act this way, nobody will like me." In the long run, hiding your authentic self can be exhausting. You might lose sight of what you genuinely enjoy or believe. This can contribute to depression because you never feel truly at ease. It is important to remember that real friendships and relationships are based on honesty. Trying to fit in at all costs can lead you away from the people who would appreciate you as you are.

---

16. Separation from Loved Ones

At times, being separated from loved ones can weigh on your heart. This might happen if a parent moves away or if family members live far apart. You could also feel separated if a close friend moves or if you lose someone who has been a big part of your life. Distance, whether physical or emotional, can lead to a sense of emptiness.

Teens who have a parent in the military, for example, might face long periods without seeing them. Others might have to live with different relatives because of financial or legal reasons. These disruptions can weaken the support network a teen depends on. If you find yourself missing important people, it can help to stay in touch however you can—calls, letters, or online messages. While it is not the same as being together in person, remaining connected can help prevent feelings of isolation that might spark depression.

17. Self-Doubt and Fear of Failure

A strong sense of self-doubt can act like a roadblock in life. You might feel like you will fail at everything you attempt, so you do not try at all. This fear can be linked to early experiences, like someone telling you that you would not succeed, or a past situation where you failed and felt embarrassed. Over time, you might develop a belief that you are less capable than other people.

This fear of failure can keep you from setting goals or taking healthy risks. It can also grow into persistent sadness if you feel stuck where you are, unable to move forward. Each day, the self-doubt can eat at your confidence, making you believe negative thoughts about your abilities. Finding small successes can help break this pattern. It might mean starting with something manageable, like learning a simple skill or joining a low-pressure activity. Success in small steps can slowly chip away at the idea that you cannot do anything right.

18. Feeling Disconnected from Activities or Purpose

Teens often want to feel that they have a place in the world. If you have not found something that makes your life feel fulfilling, you might start to feel empty. This emptiness can come if you do not enjoy school, do not have hobbies that interest you, or do not have a solid connection with friends or family. Some teens struggle to see the point of their everyday activities, leading them to question why they bother getting out of bed.

Feeling disconnected can worsen if you have tried a few clubs or sports but did not feel that you belonged. The sense of, "I have no role," can make you think you do not matter. Depression can grow in that space, telling you there is no reason to try. If this is how you feel, it might help to look for something that fits your strengths or to speak with a counselor who can help you find fresh paths. Sometimes, discovering an interest or skill can provide a sense of purpose.

19. Lack of Coping Skills

Life brings setbacks and disappointments to everyone. Teens who lack healthy coping skills might find it harder to bounce back from these setbacks. If you do not know how to handle stress, rejection, or confusion, you might internalize those feelings until they become overwhelming. Some teens turn to unhealthy coping methods, such as substance use or self-harm, which can spiral into bigger problems.

Building coping skills can be a safeguard against depression. These skills might include problem-solving techniques, relaxation exercises, or seeking support from others. When you learn healthy ways to deal with challenges, you reduce the chance that stress will accumulate to the point where it triggers depression. Coping skills do not remove problems, but they help you respond to them in a way that preserves your mental well-being.

20. A Mix of Different Influences

Often, more than one factor works together to create a situation where depression can take hold. For example, a teen might have a parent with a history of depression, live in a high-conflict household, and also face bullying at school. That combination of factors can be much more powerful than any single issue by itself. When many stressors pile up, the teen might feel overwhelmed or see no way out.

It is important to understand that not everyone is equally affected by each factor. Some teens might face significant challenges but not fall into depression, while others might develop depression with fewer apparent triggers. Each person's emotional makeup is different. The good news is that knowing about these factors can help you spot potential trouble early. If you notice several of them in your life, you can act to seek support before sadness becomes severe.

Taking Steps to Address the Factors

If you see any of these factors affecting you, it might be time to reach out for help or make changes. That could involve:

- **Talking to a Professional:** A counselor or therapist can help you understand why certain factors are affecting you and how to work around or through them.
- **Building a Support Network:** Finding friends, family members, or mentors who understand your situation can ease the feeling of being alone.
- **Adjusting Your Environment (If Possible):** If home is stressful, spend more time in activities outside the house or in spaces that feel calm. If your friend group causes you distress, you might choose to spend time with different people.
- **Exploring Coping Skills:** Learn stress-reducing techniques, time management, or other tools that help you handle life's challenges more effectively.

Knowing what contributes to depression does not solve it instantly. But it gives you a clearer picture of why you might feel the way you do. This understanding can be a key motivator to get the right help at the right time. Recognizing risk factors allows you to be more proactive. You can watch for signs of worsening sadness and catch them earlier. That way, you might prevent a mild low mood from developing into something more serious.

Conclusion

Depression can be fueled by many factors: genetics, stressful environments, personal traits, past experiences, and more. No matter which factors apply to you, remember that you are not at fault for feeling depressed. You did not choose your genes, your home life, or the hardships that came your way. What you can choose, however, is how to respond once you realize you are at risk or already feeling low.

Chapter 4: Understanding Feelings and Emotions

Feelings and emotions are a big part of what makes us human. They add color to our experiences, guide our choices, and help us connect with others. But during the teen years, emotions can sometimes feel wild or confusing. Understanding your emotions, why they happen, and how to handle them can be a powerful way to lower the risk of depression or other emotional problems. This chapter will discuss what emotions are, how they differ from thoughts, and ways to manage them in healthy ways.

---

1. What Are Emotions?

Emotions are natural responses that your mind and body create when you notice or think about something. They can show up as happiness, sadness, anger, fear, or a wide range of other states. Emotions are not random; they usually have a cause, even if that cause is not always clear right away.

For example, if you see someone laugh at you in class, you might suddenly feel anger or embarrassment. If someone surprises you with a gift, you may feel happy or touched. Emotions can also come from inside your mind, like when you remember a pleasant memory or worry about a future event. It is helpful to remember that emotions are not good or bad by themselves. They are signals that can tell you something about what is happening in your life.

---

2. How Emotions Differ from Thoughts

Though they are closely linked, emotions and thoughts are not the same thing. A **thought** is like a sentence in your mind—something you tell yourself about what is going on. An **emotion** is the feeling that comes along with it. For instance, if you see a spider and think, "That spider could harm me," your mind might produce fear. That fear is an emotional response. The thought triggers the emotion, but they are two different aspects of your experience.

Sometimes, we mix the two. We might say, "I feel like nobody likes me," but that might be a thought disguised as a feeling. The actual emotion could be sadness or worry. If we understand the difference, we can better address what is going on inside us. Knowing you are having a fearful thought can help you question it, while recognizing you are afraid can let you calm your body. This matters because if we treat a thought as a feeling, we might miss the chance to challenge that thought and see if it is true.

3. Why Emotions Can Feel Intense in Teen Years

During the teenage years, your brain undergoes significant changes. Parts of the brain that handle logic and emotional control are still growing. Hormones can also rise and fall in new ways, causing stronger emotional reactions. This means you might experience sadness, happiness, or anger more powerfully than you did as a child.

Teens also face new social and personal challenges. You might be forming your identity, dealing with peer pressure, or thinking about your future. These unknowns can stir up more complex feelings. It is not unusual to feel like you are on an emotional roller coaster. At times, these intense feelings can leave you confused, drained, or overwhelmed.

4. The Purpose of Emotions

Emotions might sometimes feel like a hassle, but they have a purpose. They can tell you when something matters to you or when something is not right. For example:

- **Fear** helps you notice danger.
- **Sadness** can show that you have lost something important or need comfort.
- **Anger** might alert you that you feel disrespected or hurt.
- **Happiness** can show that you are doing something meaningful or enjoyable.

When you understand why you feel a certain way, you can use that information. Fear might tell you to be careful in a risky situation, sadness might tell you to seek support, and anger might tell you to stand up for yourself or fix a wrong.

While it is possible to react in unhealthy ways, the emotion itself can be a helpful signal if you learn to listen to it properly.

5. Common Emotions Linked to Depression

When someone is dealing with depression, certain emotions tend to show up more often. These include:

- **Sadness:** A deep, persistent sorrow that does not seem to end.
- **Hopelessness:** Feeling as if nothing good can happen in the future.
- **Guilt:** Blaming yourself for things that might be out of your control.
- **Emptiness:** A hollow feeling, as if nothing matters or excites you.

These emotions can be powerful and stick around for weeks or months. If you notice them in yourself, try to see them as signs that you may need help or a change in what you are doing. Recognizing them early can stop them from deepening.

6. Learning to Name Your Emotions

A helpful first step in handling emotions is simply naming them. This is sometimes called "labeling." For instance, if you feel a tightness in your chest and your thoughts are racing, you might realize that you are feeling anxious. By giving a name to your emotion, you gain a bit of control over it. You move from "I'm just upset" to "I'm anxious because of the test tomorrow." This clarity can make a big difference.

If you are not sure what you are feeling, you can try to list possibilities. Ask yourself questions like: "Do I feel angry? Do I feel sad? Is there any excitement or worry mixed in?" Sometimes, you might even have more than one emotion at once, such as both anger and sadness. Putting your emotions into words can feel hard at first, but it gets easier with practice.

7. Accepting Emotions Without Judging Them

We sometimes think certain emotions are "bad" and should be ignored. For instance, you might think it is bad to feel anger because it can lead to fights. Or you might feel weak for being sad. However, judging yourself for having an emotion can make it stronger. If you tell yourself, "I should not feel this way," you add a layer of guilt on top of whatever you are already feeling.

A more helpful approach is to say, "I notice that I'm feeling angry (or sad, or anxious). That is okay. Emotions happen." This does not mean you allow yourself to act out in harmful ways, but you give yourself permission to feel. By accepting the emotion, you can examine it calmly and decide what to do next. Pushing it away often leads it to come back stronger later.

---

8. Handling Strong Emotions in Healthy Ways

There are many strategies you can use to handle strong emotions. Here are a few:

1. **Breathing Exercises:** Taking slow, deep breaths can calm your body and mind. Inhale for a count of four, hold for a count of four, and exhale for a count of four. This lowers your heart rate and can give you space to think clearly.
2. **Grounding Techniques:** These techniques help bring you back to the present moment. For example, you might pick an object and describe it in detail: its color, shape, texture, and so on. This action pulls your focus away from racing thoughts or overwhelming feelings.
3. **Physical Activity:** Moving your body can help let out built-up tension. Going for a walk, playing a sport, or even dancing in your room can provide relief. Physical movement causes your body to release chemicals that can improve mood.
4. **Talking to Someone:** Sharing your emotions with a trusted person can help you feel understood and less alone. This person might be a friend, a relative, or a counselor. Sometimes, speaking your emotions out loud helps you see them more clearly.
5. **Creative Outlets:** Drawing, writing, or playing an instrument are healthy ways to channel emotions. You do not have to be good at these activities

to benefit from them. They allow you to express yourself and process how you feel.
6. **Relaxation Practices:** Activities like taking a warm bath, listening to soothing music, or doing gentle stretches can help release tension. Over time, these small habits can make a big difference in how you handle daily stress.

---

9. Distinguishing Between Healthy and Unhealthy Emotional Responses

Not all emotional responses are helpful. For example, if you are angry, it is normal to feel that emotion, but lashing out at others can create more harm. Understanding the difference between feeling an emotion and acting on it is crucial. Feeling sad is valid, but coping by harming yourself is not helpful in the long run. You deserve healthier ways to handle pain.

One way to check if a response is healthy is to ask, "Am I making choices that help me feel better in a lasting way, or am I just trying to escape the feeling right now?" If you are turning to harmful behaviors (like substance use or aggression), you might need extra help learning alternative ways to react.

---

10. Emotions Versus Emotional Habits

Sometimes, what feels like an emotion might actually be a habit. For example, if you have been treated badly in the past, you might automatically feel anger whenever someone disagrees with you, even if they are not being unkind. This learned pattern becomes your default response. Another example is if you always assume the worst when facing a new challenge, you might slip into sadness or worry out of habit.

Breaking these emotional habits takes time and practice. First, you need to see that you might be reacting automatically. Then you can pause and try a new response. Over time, you can replace unhealthy reactions with healthier ones, but it helps to have support from friends, family, or a counselor.

11. The Importance of Self-Compassion

Self-compassion means treating yourself with the same kindness you would offer a close friend. If a friend feels sad or embarrassed about something, you might comfort them with gentle words. But if you are the one who is sad or embarrassed, you might think harsh thoughts about yourself. This habit can make negative emotions grow.

By practicing self-compassion, you learn to respond to your own pain or mistakes with understanding. This does not mean letting yourself off the hook if you do something wrong, but it means you do not sink into constant self-blame. Telling yourself, "I made a mistake, but I am still worthy of kindness," can help reduce hopelessness or guilt. Many people find that learning self-compassion is an ongoing process that takes regular effort.

---

12. Recognizing Emotional Triggers

An emotional trigger is anything that sets off a strong emotional reaction. Triggers can include situations, certain people, or even memories. For instance, you might feel deep sadness if you hear a particular song that reminds you of a hard time in your life. Or you might become instantly tense when you see a person who once bullied you.

Knowing your triggers can help you prepare. You might decide to avoid them if possible. If you cannot avoid them, you can plan ways to cope when they appear. This might include practicing breathing exercises beforehand or having a supportive friend ready to help you through it. Recognizing triggers allows you to have some control over how you respond, rather than being blindsided by intense feelings.

---

13. Emotional Expression and Communication

Sometimes, teens do not share their emotions because they fear being judged, teased, or misunderstood. But keeping everything inside can worsen negative feelings. Healthy emotional expression often means saying, "I feel upset because of what happened," rather than acting out or pretending nothing is wrong.

When talking to someone about how you feel, try to use "I" statements. For example, "I feel hurt when I'm ignored," is clearer and less accusing than "You always ignore me!" Using "I" statements can help the other person understand your feelings without feeling attacked. This can lead to calmer, more productive conversations.

14. How Emotional Awareness Helps Prevent Depression

Emotional awareness is your ability to notice and understand your feelings. This skill can help keep you from sinking into deep depression. When you are in touch with your emotions, you are less likely to bury them or let them grow unchecked. Instead, you can address them before they spiral into something bigger.

For example, if you notice you are feeling lonely, you can take steps to reach out to a friend or join a club. If you notice you are feeling bored or unmotivated, you might try a new activity or talk to a mentor about how to set fresh goals. By spotting and naming these feelings early, you reduce the chance that they will turn into prolonged sadness or hopelessness.

15. Balancing Emotions in Everyday Life

It is normal for your emotions to go up and down over the course of a day or week. Sometimes, you might feel like you are doing great. Other times, small setbacks can cause your emotions to drop. Balance does not mean being cheerful all the time. It means learning how to handle the lows without letting them destroy your overall hope.

Here are a few tips for seeking balance:

1. **Plan Enjoyable Activities:** Try to do at least one pleasant or interesting activity each day, even if it is something small like listening to a favorite song or doodling in a notebook.
2. **Practice Gratitude:** Focusing on a few things you appreciate can shift your mood. You might list them in your mind before bed or write them in a small journal.

3. **Limit Overthinking:** If you catch yourself spiraling in negative thoughts, try to redirect your attention to something more grounding, like a task or a breathing exercise.
4. **Stay Connected:** Talk to someone you trust regularly. Being heard and understood can help you stay level when your feelings get strong.

---

16. Emotions in Relationships

Whether it is a friendship, a family relationship, or a romantic connection, emotions can play a huge role. When you have strong feelings for someone, disagreements can feel more intense. Feelings of jealousy or fear of being left out can also come up. Learning to handle your emotions in these situations is important. Good communication can stop misunderstandings from growing into larger arguments or long-term resentments.

It can help to talk openly about emotional needs with the people in your life. You might say, "When you interrupt me, I feel upset because I think my words are not important." This might feel awkward at first, but it helps others understand what you are experiencing. Healthy relationships involve sharing, listening, and respecting each other's feelings.

---

17. Building Emotional Resilience

Emotional resilience means being able to bounce back when you face stress or disappointment. People who are resilient still feel sadness or worry, but they have learned ways to recover and adapt. You can build resilience by practicing the skills we have talked about—naming your emotions, using coping strategies, and seeking support. Resilience is not something you either have or do not have; it can be improved with effort over time.

Taking small steps to improve your self-esteem can also support resilience. This might include celebrating small victories (like completing a difficult project) and reminding yourself that you are capable of learning new things. Feeling good about your own abilities can keep you steady when tough emotions arise.

18. When Emotions Become Overwhelming

Sometimes, emotions can feel like they are too big to handle. You might cry for hours, lash out at people around you, or feel frozen in place. If you often feel overwhelmed or find it difficult to control your responses, this may point to deeper problems like anxiety, depression, or past trauma that needs professional attention. That is okay—it just means you might benefit from extra support.

Signs that your emotions might be too strong to handle alone include:

- You have severe mood swings that come out of nowhere.
- You find yourself getting angry or sad multiple times a day, every day.
- You avoid activities or people because you are afraid of losing control.
- You do things to hurt yourself or feel the urge to.

If this is your experience, talking to a mental health professional can be a big help. You are not weak for needing that level of care. Instead, it takes courage to face your emotions head-on and seek solutions.

---

19. The Role of Mindfulness

Mindfulness is the practice of paying close attention to what you feel, think, and sense right now, without judging it. You can practice mindfulness in many ways, such as by focusing on your breathing or noticing each part of your body. Doing this regularly can help you become more aware of your emotions early on, before they grow too big.

For example, if you begin to notice your heart rate speeding up and your jaw clenching, you might realize you are becoming anxious. By catching it early, you can apply a calming strategy right away. Mindfulness also helps you notice negative thought patterns as they begin, letting you question them rather than just accepting them as true. Many teens find that simple, short mindfulness exercises can lower daily stress and keep their emotions more balanced.

20. Accepting Help

Finally, never forget that you do not have to handle your emotions alone. Reaching out for help can happen in many forms: talking to family, seeking counseling, joining a support group, or finding an online community that understands what you are feeling. Some schools have programs or clubs where students support each other's mental health.

Needing help is normal, especially if your emotions are strong and confusing. The main point is not to keep quiet. Let at least one person know how you feel. By opening up, you create the chance for solutions, advice, or empathy that you might not find if you try to manage everything inside your own head.

Conclusion

Emotions are powerful forces in our lives. They let us know what matters, guide our decisions, and help us connect to other people. During the teen years, these emotions can feel overpowering or baffling at times, especially when combined with the pressures and changes of adolescence. However, by learning to understand, name, and respond to your emotions in healthy ways, you can avoid letting them spiral out of control.

This chapter has shown that emotions themselves are not dangerous, but the way we respond to them can either help us or harm us. If we understand that emotions serve a purpose and can be managed, we take a big step toward protecting our mental health. This understanding is one part of preventing or dealing with depression. The more you learn to handle and accept your emotions, the easier it will be to spot signs of deeper sadness or hopelessness. You will also be better able to talk about them with others and find the support you need.

Chapter 5: Reaching Out for Help

When you feel depressed or overwhelmed, it can be hard to share your struggles with anyone. You might think nobody will care or that you should handle it alone. It is important to know that reaching out for help can make a difference. You do not have to go through depression on your own, and there are many people and resources that can support you. This chapter will cover why it is helpful to seek assistance, the kinds of support that are available, and how to take the first steps toward telling someone what you are going through.

---

1. Why Asking for Help Matters

Depression thrives on isolation. When you feel hopeless or sad, you might think, "Nobody wants to hear about my problems," or "I should be able to handle this on my own." But these thoughts can keep you trapped. Talking about your feelings with someone you trust can lessen the weight you carry. You might feel relief just knowing that another person is listening without judging you.

Support is also key in addressing depression before it grows worse. The sooner you seek help, the more quickly you can find useful tools or treatments. If you hurt your knee while playing sports, you would likely see a doctor. If your mind hurts from sad or hopeless thoughts, seeking help from a mental health professional or a supportive adult is just as important. Depression is a real condition that benefits from care.

---

2. Recognizing Barriers to Seeking Help

Many teens do not ask for help because of fear, stigma, or shame. They might worry they will be labeled as "weak" or "dramatic." They might fear being judged by classmates, friends, or relatives. Sometimes, teens worry that talking about mental health problems will lead to conflict at home or cause parents to be upset. These concerns are valid, but remember that depression is a health issue, just like any physical ailment.

Another barrier is not knowing where to turn. You might feel lost about who to trust or how to explain what you are experiencing. If you feel this way, you are not alone. Lots of people do not know where to begin, but once you identify a starting point, it can become easier to take the next step.

---

3. Choosing Someone to Talk To

Picking the right person to talk to can be an important decision. You might consider:

1. **Parents or Guardians:** If you have a caring relationship with your parents or guardians, they can be a strong source of support. They may not always know the right words, but they can help you reach professionals or make changes in your routine to lessen your stress.
2. **Trusted Relatives:** If speaking with your parents is not an option, you could look to another adult in your family, such as an aunt, uncle, or older cousin. They might offer a listening ear and help you find resources.
3. **School Counselors or Teachers:** Many schools have counselors who are trained to help students facing emotional challenges. A teacher you trust can also guide you to the right offices or people at school.
4. **Close Friends:** A supportive friend can help you feel less alone. Friends might share their own experiences or simply be there to listen when you want to talk. While friends may not replace professional help, they can still be a comforting presence.
5. **Community Leaders or Mentors:** Depending on your situation, you might find guidance from a leader in your community or a mentor you respect. They might have experience helping young people and can keep conversations confidential.

If you worry about how an adult will react, you can test the waters by mentioning that you have been feeling very down. Notice if they respond with kindness. If they seem open, you can consider telling them more. If they do not respond well, it is okay to seek someone else.

4. Professional Support: Therapists and Counselors

A mental health professional, such as a therapist or counselor, has studied ways to help people work through challenges like depression. Talking with them can feel awkward at first, especially if you have never been in therapy. Over time, you may discover that it is a safe place to talk about your worries, fears, or painful experiences without judgment.

Therapists can help you understand why you feel the way you do and teach you skills to handle sad or negative thoughts. For example, they might show you how to reframe discouraging ideas, manage stress, or practice healthy communication. They are bound by rules that require them to keep your conversations private, except in cases where your safety or another person's safety is at risk.

5. Psychiatrists and Medication

Some teens might work with a psychiatrist if their depression is severe or does not get better with therapy alone. Psychiatrists are medical doctors who can decide if medication could help with depression. Medication can adjust certain brain chemicals to lessen deep sadness or hopelessness. However, it is not a "quick fix." Medicines can take time to work, and they can have side effects. It is important to keep open communication with the doctor about how you feel if you do try medication.

Medication is never the only solution. It often goes hand in hand with therapy and lifestyle changes. Still, for some people, it can be a helpful part of a plan to manage depression. If you or your parents have concerns about medication, talk honestly with the psychiatrist about the risks and benefits. You have a right to understand your treatment choices.

6. Hotlines and Crisis Text Lines

If you ever feel like you might harm yourself or you are in a crisis, there are hotlines and text lines you can use to talk to someone right away. These services are usually confidential and are there to help you get through the immediate danger. They can also guide you to resources near you. You do not need permission from anyone to reach out to these hotlines. They exist so that young people can have a lifeline in their hardest moments.

Examples could include:

- Phone hotlines that let you speak with a trained listener.
- Text lines where you can share your thoughts via messages if you do not want to speak on the phone.

If you do not know the hotline numbers in your area, you can look them up online or ask a school counselor for the information ahead of time. Even if you are not sure you are in crisis, but you feel unsafe inside your mind, it is okay to reach out.

7. Online Support and Groups

Online communities can be a good place to find information, share feelings, and connect with others who have had similar experiences. However, you should be careful about what sites or groups you join. Not all online spaces are safe or helpful. Some might have misinformation, and others could encourage harmful behavior. If you decide to look for online support, try to find forums or groups moderated by mental health professionals or known organizations.

Keep your personal information private, especially in public forums. Also, if an online space makes you feel worse or is filled with negative comments, it is okay to leave and look for a better option. Online support can be a starting point, but it often works best when used along with real-life support from counselors, doctors, or friends you can trust in person.

8. Peer Support Programs

Some schools have peer support programs where students are trained to help classmates who feel sad, stressed, or anxious. If your school offers such a program, you might find it easier to talk to a peer counselor because they are closer to your age. They might relate to your problems and worries more directly. Peer counselors usually learn about listening skills and how to keep what you say private. They can also give you tips on handling school pressures or direct you to an adult counselor for more serious issues.

9. How to Start the Conversation

For many teens, the hardest part is starting that first conversation. You might rehearse in your head a hundred times what to say but still feel uneasy. Here are a few tips:

1. **Write It Down:** If speaking aloud feels intimidating, try writing a brief note or email. You can hand it to the person you trust or send it, explaining that you have been feeling low and need someone to talk to.
2. **Practice an Opener:** For instance, say, "There's been a lot on my mind lately. I could use someone to talk to. Is now a good time?" This simple question can help you see if the person is ready to listen.
3. **Use Technology:** If a face-to-face talk seems too difficult at first, a text or voice message might help you open up. Later, you can meet in person when you feel more comfortable.
4. **Be Direct if You Can:** Try statements like, "I think I might be depressed," or "I'm really struggling with sadness." Sometimes being clear about how serious you feel can signal to the other person that you need more than a casual chat.

10. Dealing with Reactions

People react in different ways when they learn someone they care about is feeling depressed. Some might show worry right away and offer support. Others might be silent because they do not know what to say. A few might react with disbelief or say something hurtful out of ignorance, like "You're just being lazy," or "Snap out of it." If someone reacts poorly, try not to let it stop you from seeking help. It might mean you need to find a better listener.

If the person you share with gets upset or blames themselves, try to stay calm. You can let them know you are not blaming them, but you need their understanding. If they do not calm down or remain upset, it may be best to find someone else to talk to who can stay focused on your needs.

11. Keeping Communication Open

Reaching out once is an important first step, but staying in touch with your support network is also useful. Depression can come and go in waves. If you stop talking after one conversation, you might find yourself feeling isolated again later. Checking in with the same trusted person or professional from time to time can help you keep track of your feelings, celebrate small signs of progress, and catch warning signs of deeper sadness. If therapy or counseling is part of your plan, regular appointments can give you a stable place to share updates.

12. Handling Confidentiality Concerns

Many teens worry that if they tell an adult about their depression, their problems will become public knowledge. In most cases, counselors, therapists, and doctors keep your information private. They only share details if they think you are in serious danger or if they must by law. Teachers, coaches, and other adults might not have strict confidentiality rules, but often they will keep sensitive information to themselves unless there is a risk to your safety.

If you have questions about how confidentiality works, ask the person you are talking to about their guidelines. This can help you feel safer. If you find that the rules in your situation are not strict enough, you might seek out a professional counselor or therapist who has to follow clear privacy rules.

13. Group Therapy and Support Groups

Some teens benefit from group therapy or in-person support groups where people share their stories and coping techniques. Being in a room (or virtual space) with others who face depression can make you feel less alone. In group settings, you might learn new methods for dealing with sadness or hopelessness. You can also hear real-life stories about getting better.

Before you join a group, check who leads it and how they handle discussions. Ideally, it should be guided by a trained counselor who can keep conversations helpful and respectful. Group settings are not for everyone, but they can be a comforting option for those who want to connect with people who truly understand.

14. When Professional Help Feels Uncomfortable

You might meet a therapist or counselor and not feel a connection. That does not mean therapy will never work for you. People have different personalities and approaches. If you do not feel comfortable with one professional, it is okay to seek another. You want someone you can trust and open up to. It might take a few tries to find the right match.

Some teens stop going to therapy because it feels awkward or they do not see immediate results. Therapy is usually a gradual process that takes time. It involves learning about yourself, your habits, and new ways to cope. If you stick with it, many find therapy becomes easier and more useful as they build a relationship with the counselor.

15. Helping a Friend Who Is Depressed

Reaching out for help is not just about getting help for yourself. Sometimes you might notice a friend struggling. They may have changes in mood, lose interest in things they enjoyed, or talk about feeling hopeless. If you see this, consider asking gently, "How are you doing? You seem kind of down. Do you want to talk?" If they open up, you can encourage them to speak to a counselor or another adult they trust. Offer to go with them if they feel nervous.

Remember that you are not a trained professional. You can be there as a friend, but if the person is talking about harming themselves or shows serious signs of depression, it is important to tell a counselor, teacher, or parent—even if your friend begs you to keep it secret. Keeping them safe is more important than promising silence.

16. Building a Personal Support Plan

It can help to write out a plan for times when your depression feels intense. This plan might include:

- A list of safe people you can call or text (friends, relatives, hotlines).
- Activities or hobbies that usually help you calm down or feel better (listening to music, taking a short walk, reading, etc.).
- A reminder to tell a trusted adult if you have thoughts of harming yourself.
- Contact information for local mental health resources or counselors.

Keep this plan somewhere private but easy to find, like in your phone or a small notebook. The idea is that when strong feelings hit, you will not have to think too hard about what to do.

---

17. Online Therapy and Telehealth

Some counselors offer online sessions, which can be a good option if you have trouble traveling to an office or if there are not many services near you. These sessions might happen over video calls or through a counseling app. If you are more comfortable in your own room or cannot get a ride to a clinic, online therapy might help you open up. However, make sure you are using a reputable service. You should still feel that your privacy is protected, and the counselor should be licensed.

---

18. Seeking Help Does Not Make You Weak

One of the biggest myths about asking for help is that it means you are not strong enough to handle problems yourself. In reality, recognizing that you need support shows wisdom. It means you value your well-being and want to find a way to feel better. Reaching out can be an act of self-care and courage. Life is full of problems that nobody can handle alone. Building a network of caring people can allow you to face challenges with less fear and more confidence.

19. Preparing for the Possibility of Needing Long-Term Support

Depression can be complex, and it does not always vanish after a few therapy sessions. Some people find they need long-term counseling or check-ins, especially if their life circumstances are stressful or if they have a family history of depression. Others might experience depressive episodes off and on throughout their lives. If that happens, staying connected to a counselor or support group can help keep symptoms in check. With ongoing support, many teens grow into adults who manage their depression in healthy ways.

---

20. You Are Not Alone

It is common to feel alone when you are depressed. But remember, many teens have been where you are. They have reached out, found help, and are now in a better place. Even if it takes time to find the right person or approach, you deserve to be heard and to feel hope. Keep in mind that there is a system of care designed to catch people who feel they are at the end of their rope. Friends, family, therapists, teachers—they may each play a part in supporting you.

Conclusion

Reaching out for help is a vital step in dealing with teen depression. Speaking with a trusted adult, professional, or friend can lift some of the heaviness you are carrying. There are many ways to seek assistance—through school counselors, therapists, hotlines, and online resources. If one option does not work out, try another until you find a good fit. Sharing your challenges with someone who cares can help you realize you are not at fault for feeling depressed and that it is possible to regain a sense of hope. Even if it feels scary at first, taking action can steer you toward the understanding and guidance you need.

Chapter 6: Changing Unhelpful Thought Patterns

The way you think has a big effect on how you feel. When you are depressed, negative thoughts can fill your mind, making it hard to see anything good about yourself or the world. These unhelpful thoughts often happen so automatically that you do not even notice them. Changing these patterns is possible, but it takes awareness and practice. This chapter explains how to spot harmful thinking, why it matters, and what you can do to develop more balanced ways of looking at things.

1. How Thoughts Affect Feelings

Thoughts are like stories you tell yourself about what is happening or who you are. If those stories are always negative or overly critical, they can push you into a low mood or keep you stuck in sad feelings. For example:

- If you make a small mistake on a school project and think, "I'm a total failure," you may feel shame or sadness.
- If a friend cancels plans and you think, "They must hate me," you might feel angry or lonely.

The event itself (the mistake or the canceled plan) is not necessarily the main problem. It is the meaning you give to it. By learning to notice and question your thoughts, you can break free from negative loops.

2. Common Unhelpful Thinking Patterns

There are several thinking patterns, sometimes called "cognitive distortions," that can make depression worse. Recognizing these patterns is the first step toward changing them. Here are a few examples:

1. **All-or-Nothing Thinking:** Seeing things in black-and-white terms. You either do something perfectly, or you have failed. In reality, most things fall somewhere in between.

2. **Overgeneralizing:** Believing that if something bad happens once, it will happen again and again. For example, "I failed one math test, so I'll never pass any math test."
3. **Catastrophizing:** Expecting the worst outcome in every situation. You might think, "If I don't get this job, my life is over," even though there are many other options.
4. **Personalizing:** Blaming yourself for events that are not under your control. If friends argue, you might think, "It's all my fault," even if you played no role in their fight.
5. **Mind Reading:** Believing you know what others are thinking, usually assuming they have negative thoughts about you. For example, "She didn't smile at me today. She must think I'm annoying."
6. **Discounting Positives:** Ignoring or dismissing good things about yourself or your life. If someone praises you, you might think, "They're just being nice," instead of accepting the compliment as real.
7. **Labeling:** Putting a negative label on yourself or others. Instead of saying, "I made a mistake," you say, "I'm stupid."

These patterns can mix together and reinforce each other. They feel real in the moment, but they are often not accurate reflections of reality. They create a lens that makes everything look worse than it is.

---

3. Identifying Your Own Negative Thoughts

Before you can change harmful thoughts, you need to notice them. One way is to keep a journal or a note on your phone. Each time you feel a strong wave of sadness or anxiety, write down what was going through your mind at that moment. Ask yourself:

- "What did I think right before I started feeling this way?"
- "Is there a pattern in these thoughts?"
- "Do I recognize any unhelpful thinking style from the list above?"

You might be surprised at how often your mind jumps to negative conclusions. By getting these thoughts out of your head and onto paper (or a screen), you can look at them more objectively.

4. Challenging Unhelpful Thoughts

Once you identify a negative thought, try to challenge it. This does not mean denying the facts. It means checking whether your interpretation is completely true. For instance, if you wrote, "I did badly on my test, so I'll fail the entire class," ask yourself:

- Is it true that one bad test means I'll fail the class?
- Have I ever recovered from a bad grade before?
- Are there steps I can take to improve my grade from now on?

These questions help you see that the original thought was an extreme or unfair conclusion. The goal is to shift from "I'll fail for sure" to something more balanced, like, "I didn't do well on this test, but I can study differently next time. One bad grade doesn't seal my fate."

Chapter 7: Building Self-Care Habits

Taking care of yourself is important for overall well-being, especially during your teenage years when life can seem unpredictable. When you hear "self-care," you might think of activities like taking a bath or lighting a scented candle. While those can be relaxing, self-care also involves healthy routines and daily choices that help keep your mind and body strong. Building self-care habits can give you the tools to handle mood changes and stresses before they become overwhelming. This chapter will explore many sides of self-care, from physical health to emotional and social well-being, and offer suggestions you can try right away.

---

1. What Self-Care Really Means

Self-care is any practice that supports your body, mind, or emotions in a healthy way. It does not have to be fancy or cost money. Sometimes, it can be something as simple as drinking water when you are thirsty or taking a break when you feel tense. By making self-care a normal part of each day, you give yourself a better chance to stay balanced. You also have more energy to handle problems when they show up.

Many teens might view self-care as selfish, thinking, "I should be focusing on school, family, or chores instead." But looking after your own needs helps you be stronger in all areas of life. It helps you prevent feeling drained, which can lead to mood swings or deeper sadness. Proper self-care often means small steps taken regularly that add up to big improvements in how you feel.

---

2. Physical Health as a Cornerstone

Your body and mind are linked closely. When your body is cared for, it can be easier to manage your moods. Here are a few ways to pay attention to your physical health:

1. **Sleep:** Aim for about eight to ten hours each night. Teens often need more sleep than adults to support the changes in their growing bodies.

Lack of rest can affect your mood, appetite, and ability to think clearly. If you have trouble sleeping, try setting a regular bedtime and cutting back on screen use before bedtime.
2. **Movement:** Finding a way to move that you enjoy can boost your mood. It could be walking, dancing in your room, playing a sport, or riding a bike. When you get your heart rate up, your body releases chemicals that can lessen anxiety and lift your spirits. Even 15 minutes of light movement each day can make a difference.
3. **Eating Well:** Nourishing your body with a balanced mix of foods can help keep your energy levels steady. If possible, include fruits, vegetables, whole grains, and proteins in your daily meals. This does not mean you have to swear off snacks or treats entirely. It is more about being aware of what you eat and how it affects your mood. Some teens find they feel more balanced when they limit sugary drinks and high-sugar foods.
4. **Hydration:** Water is essential for every part of your body, including your brain. If you feel dizzy, weak, or unable to concentrate, you might be dehydrated. Keep a bottle of water with you during the day, especially if you live in a hot climate or do sports.
5. **Limit Harmful Substances:** Some teens might try alcohol, tobacco, or other substances to cope with stress. But these do more harm than good, especially in the long run. If you feel tempted to use substances for relief, consider looking for healthier outlets—like talking to a friend or counselor, taking a short walk, or practicing deep breathing.

By treating your body with kindness, you create a strong base for mental and emotional health. It might sound basic, but missing out on one of these areas—sleep, movement, nutrition, or hydration—can increase sadness or stress.

---

3. Emotional Self-Care

Emotional self-care means finding healthy ways to express and handle your feelings. Bottling up emotions can lead to bigger problems, while letting them out in safe ways can help you process them. Below are a few methods:

1. **Writing in a Journal:** Putting your thoughts on paper can free your mind from racing ideas. You can also track patterns—do certain events or people trigger negative feelings? Seeing it in writing might help you come up with ways to cope.

2. **Artistic Expression:** Drawing, painting, singing, or playing an instrument can be a way to release feelings that are hard to put into words. You do not need to be good at art for it to help. The point is to let your emotions flow out safely.
3. **Allowing Yourself to Cry:** Crying can be a normal reaction to sadness, anger, or frustration. It can sometimes help you feel lighter afterward. If you notice yourself on the verge of tears, find a quiet space where you feel safe to let it out without shame.
4. **Calm Breathing:** Simple breathing exercises, such as inhaling slowly through the nose for a count of four and then exhaling through the mouth for a count of four, can reduce tension. Breathing methods can be used anytime, such as before an exam or when you feel stressed at home.
5. **Naming Your Feelings:** Sometimes, simply saying, "I feel upset," or "I feel worried," can lessen the power of those emotions. It is a way of admitting they are there without judging yourself.

By tending to your emotional well-being, you can reduce the buildup of stress and sad feelings. Over time, these practices can help you see your emotions as something you can observe and handle, rather than something that overwhelms you.

---

4. Social and Environmental Self-Care

The people and surroundings in your life can either fill you with energy or drain you. Social and environmental self-care involves choosing supportive company and comfortable spaces when you can.

1. **Choosing Supportive Company:** Spend time with friends who listen, respect your boundaries, and genuinely care about how you are doing. If a friend always puts you down or ignores your feelings, it might be best to limit time with that person. The same goes for online connections. If someone's posts or messages make you feel bad, consider unfollowing or blocking them.
2. **Setting Boundaries:** Let others know what you are okay with and what makes you uncomfortable. For example, you can tell someone if you need some quiet time or if you do not want to talk about certain personal

topics. Setting clear boundaries can protect your emotional and mental health.
3. **Creating a Cozy Space:** Your bedroom or study area can influence your mood. If possible, arrange it in a way that feels calm—maybe put up a comforting photo or keep favorite items within sight. Try to keep it clean enough so that you are not stressed by clutter. A little tidying each day can keep your space more peaceful.
4. **Finding Places to Unwind:** If home is noisy or stressful, look for other places to spend time, like a public library, a quiet park, or a community center. Having a spot where you can recharge can be an important part of self-care.
5. **Connecting in Person:** Face-to-face contact can be powerful. Spending time with someone you trust, talking about everyday things, or even sitting together in comfortable silence can help you feel less alone. If you have loved ones far away, a video call can be the next best thing.

These steps might seem small, but they can help you build a safe environment and social circle. Knowing that you have a place to go and people who care can protect you from feeling overwhelmed.

---

5. Setting Realistic Goals for Self-Care

It can be tempting to try to change everything at once—exercise daily, eat perfect meals, and write in a journal every morning. But aiming too high too fast can lead to burnout. Instead, try setting a few small, realistic goals:

- **Pick One Physical Habit:** For example, decide to go to sleep 15 minutes earlier than you usually do.
- **Choose One Emotional Habit:** Write a short note each evening about one thing you felt grateful for during the day.
- **Plan One Social Action:** Send a supportive text to a friend or plan a short meetup once a week.

By starting small, you can see success right away. Success can encourage you to keep going. Over time, you can add new goals or expand on the ones that work well. This approach prevents you from feeling guilty if you cannot keep up with a long list of changes.

6. How Self-Care Helps Fight Depression

When you are feeling depressed, it can be tough to get excited about caring for yourself. Doing self-care might feel like a chore. But these small acts help you keep a connection to your body, your feelings, and your interests. Even if you cannot make yourself feel cheerful right away, self-care can stop the slide into deeper sadness by providing structure and giving you a sense of control over some parts of your day.

For instance, a teen who schedules a short walk each morning might notice that getting outside lifts their mood slightly. This boost can make it a bit easier to face the day. Another teen might find that journaling every night helps them see patterns in their sadness and identify triggers. Over time, these habits can lead to big changes in how they cope with difficult emotions.

---

7. Keeping Self-Care Simple

Sometimes, the word "routine" can sound like a big commitment. If you are already feeling low, you might not have the motivation to create an elaborate plan. That is okay. Self-care can be simple:

- **Have a Glass of Water:** Before you check your phone in the morning, drink a glass of water. It might seem small, but it starts your day with a helpful action.
- **Stretch for One Minute:** A few simple stretches for your arms, neck, or back can help your body wake up.
- **Breathe in Fresh Air:** If you can, step outside for a moment, even if it is just on your doorstep. Notice the temperature, the sky, or the sounds around you.
- **Pick One Task to Complete:** Feeling overwhelmed? Choose one thing—like picking up clothes off your floor or replying to one email—and do it. This small achievement can give you a bit of energy to do the next thing.

The key is to find at least one tiny step you can handle, even on a tough day. Having these options ready can help you feel less overwhelmed when your mood dips.

8. Mixing Self-Care with Fun

Self-care is not all about chores. It can also be fun activities that bring you some enjoyment or relaxation. Maybe you like reading comics, playing a musical instrument, or playing a casual video game. If it helps you feel calmer or recharged, it can count as self-care. The idea is to do it mindfully. That means you focus on what you are doing rather than worrying about everything else. You can set aside a short time each day—maybe 15 minutes—to do something just for you.

Try not to feel guilty about taking breaks to do things you like. Short breaks can help you refocus on chores or homework afterward. The key is balance—too much time doing fun stuff might lead to stress later if responsibilities stack up, but a little time each day to do something you enjoy can keep your mood steadier.

---

9. Handling Guilt Over Self-Care

Some teens feel guilty spending time on themselves, especially if they have many duties at home or school. They might think, "I should be helping out instead of relaxing." However, taking short breaks to look after your mind and body can help you be a better student, family member, or friend in the long run. When your own energy is drained, you have less to give to others. If you struggle with guilt, remind yourself that self-care is not laziness. It is a way to make sure you stay healthy and capable.

If you really cannot find time due to responsibilities, try blending self-care with tasks. For example, you can do some light stretches while waiting for dinner to cook, or take a few deep breaths while standing in line. These small moments can recharge you without taking away from other duties.

---

10. Digital Self-Care

Many teens spend hours each day online. While the internet can be helpful for school and connecting with friends, it can also become overwhelming. Here are some ways to practice digital self-care:

1. **Set Time Limits:** Some phones allow you to set daily limits on apps. If you often lose track of time on social media, these limits can remind you to take a break.
2. **Follow Positive Content:** If your feed is full of negative comments or people who make you feel bad about yourself, consider unfollowing them. Instead, follow pages or individuals who are uplifting or informative in a good way.
3. **Screen-Free Periods:** Try going without your phone or computer for a short part of each day, like during meals or right before bed. This can help you relax and be present in the moment.
4. **Pay Attention to Your Emotions Online:** If scrolling makes you feel anxious or upset, it might be a sign that you need to step away. Closing an app or stepping away from the screen for a bit can protect your mood.

Digital self-care is about taking control of how you use technology rather than letting it control you. It can be a challenge at first if you are used to checking your phone often, but even a few small breaks can help clear your mind.

---

11. Building a Self-Care Toolkit

It can help to have a "toolkit" of self-care ideas ready for days when you feel down. This toolkit could be a physical box or just a list in your phone. In it, you can include:

- **Calming Activities:** Such as coloring pages, a short puzzle, or instructions for a breathing exercise.
- **Comfort Items:** Maybe a soft blanket, a stress ball, or a favorite photo that makes you smile.
- **Positive Quotes or Notes:** Write down kind words for yourself to read when you feel upset.
- **Contact Numbers:** List phone numbers of friends, family, or hotlines you trust.

When you feel overwhelmed, you can look at your toolkit and pick something to try. Having it prepared ahead of time means you do not have to think too hard when your mood is low.

12. Knowing When Self-Care Is Not Enough

Self-care can help protect your mental health, but it is not a substitute for professional support if you are dealing with serious depression. If you have been trying self-care habits and still feel constant sadness, hopelessness, or have thoughts of harming yourself, it is important to reach out for help. This might mean talking to a counselor, doctor, or someone you trust. Self-care is only one part of a bigger set of supports you might need. There is no shame in needing more than just daily routines to feel okay.

---

13. Balancing Self-Care and Other Priorities

You might wonder how to fit self-care into a busy schedule with school, chores, or a job. Balancing these can be tough, but it is possible. A few ideas:

- **Use Spare Moments:** If you have short breaks during the school day, you can use them to take a few deep breaths, do a quick stretch, or jot down a quick journal note.
- **Focus on Weekends or Days Off:** If weekday schedules are packed, set aside a little more time on weekends to do something comforting—like a walk in the park or a nice breakfast.
- **Combine Self-Care with Tasks:** Listen to relaxing music or an audiobook while doing chores. This way, you still finish your duties but also have a calmer mind.
- **Plan Ahead:** If you know you have a big test or project, schedule your time so you do not have to stay up all night. This helps you avoid excessive stress that can hurt your mood.

The idea is not to ignore responsibilities but to weave in self-care when you can. Even small breaks can protect your mental health in the middle of busy days.

---

14. Trying Different Methods

Not every self-care method will work for everyone. Some teens prefer active outlets like running or dancing, while others find peace in writing or drawing. You might try a new method—like mindfulness or guided relaxation—and realize it does not help. That is okay. The key is to keep experimenting until you find several methods that fit your personality and lifestyle.

It can help to talk to friends or family members about what they do to relax and recharge. You could get new ideas and decide to try them. The important thing is to be open-minded. You might discover an approach you never thought you would like, such as gardening or cooking, and it becomes a helpful self-care habit.

---

15. Involving Friends or Family in Self-Care

Self-care does not always have to be a solo activity. Sometimes, sharing the experience with others can make it more fun and help you stick to it. For example, you could:

- **Walk with a Friend:** Make a plan to walk around your neighborhood together a few times a week.
- **Cook a Simple Meal with a Family Member:** This can teach you a new recipe while also providing some bonding time.
- **Have a Quiet Study Session:** If schoolwork is stressful, invite a friend over and study in a calm environment. Breaks can include short stretches or snack time.
- **Organize a Craft Night:** Get together with a few friends and do art or crafts. This can be relaxing and a chance to express yourself.

Doing self-care with others can help you stay motivated. It also allows you to build relationships and foster a sense of support, which is another important part of mental well-being.

---

16. Mindful Use of Relaxing Apps or Music

Many phone apps offer guided relaxation, sleep stories, or calming music. These can be helpful tools if used in moderation. For instance, you could listen to soothing sounds before bedtime to wind down. Or you might use a guided relaxation app to help you breathe better when you feel anxious.

Make sure the app or music fits your needs. Some apps might be too busy or distracting, while others may feel just right. If an app encourages self-harm or negative thinking, it is not a good choice. Always trust your gut feeling: if it helps you feel calmer, it might be worth keeping; if it increases your worries, it is best to move on to something else.

17. Tracking Your Progress

Watching your progress can show you which self-care steps are having the most impact. You could use a habit tracker, mark a calendar, or just note how you feel each day after practicing a self-care activity. Over time, you might see patterns—like noticing that you feel calmer on days when you do a short morning stretch or when you spend fewer hours on social media.

Seeing improvement, even small shifts in mood or energy, can motivate you to continue. If you do not see any change after a while, you can switch up your methods. It is a trial-and-error process, and that is normal. You are learning what works best for your unique needs.

18. Overcoming Obstacles to Self-Care

Sometimes, you might know what self-care actions would help, but you still do not do them. This can happen for many reasons—lack of time, lack of energy, or even feeling you do not deserve to feel better. If you notice that you keep putting off self-care, try to identify why. Are you too tired? Do you feel guilty about it? Once you know the reason, you can address it:

- **Too Tired:** If you are low on energy, pick very small steps, like taking just a five-minute break or choosing one simple thing you can manage.
- **Feeling Guilty:** Remind yourself that caring for yourself helps you be kinder and more present for others.
- **Forgetting:** Set an alarm on your phone or leave a note on your desk to remind you.

Overcoming these obstacles might take time, but small adjustments can help you include self-care in your regular life.

19. Connecting Self-Care with Bigger Goals

Sometimes, tying self-care to things that matter to you can boost motivation. For example, if you want to do better in sports, you can focus on sleep and good nutrition to have more energy. If you care about being there for your friends, you can focus on managing stress so you will not be irritable or distant. Linking self-care to your values makes it feel more meaningful, rather than just another chore on your to-do list.

20. Looking Ahead

Building self-care habits is a long-term project, not a one-time fix. As you go through your teen years, your needs might change. What helps you relax at 14 might be different from what helps at 17. Stay open to adjusting your routines. Self-care is about being kind to yourself and recognizing that your mental and physical health deserve attention.

By learning to care for yourself in small daily ways, you become more resilient against depression. You also set a pattern for life—treating yourself with respect, investing in your well-being, and balancing responsibilities with rest and kindness. The next time you feel a dip in your mood, remember that self-care is there to help lift you back up, one simple step at a time.

Chapter 8: Managing Stress in Everyday Life

Stress is part of life, but too much of it can fuel feelings of depression or anxiety. Many teens juggle school demands, social pressures, family responsibilities, and sometimes jobs. When stress piles up, it can feel like you are always on edge, unable to relax or enjoy anything. This chapter will look at ways to manage everyday stress so that it does not overwhelm you. We will talk about recognizing stress signals, making healthy choices, and adopting habits that help keep your mind steady even when life gets hectic.

1. Understanding Stress

Stress is your body's reaction to challenges or demands. It can come from events at school, arguments with friends, or even personal worries about the future. Some stress can be helpful—it might push you to study for a test or meet a deadline. But when stress becomes constant, it can wear down your mind and body. You might have trouble sleeping, feel more impatient, or lose interest in things that used to bring you pleasure.

A key step is realizing that you have stress. Sometimes, teens get so used to feeling pressured that they think it is normal. But ongoing stress can contribute to headaches, tense muscles, stomach problems, and a lowered immune system. It can also make you more prone to deep sadness. Recognizing that stress is present can help you take action.

2. Common Sources of Teen Stress

Teens can face stress from many areas, such as:

1. **Academic Pressure:** Tests, projects, essays, and the belief that you must get high grades or get into a particular school can create ongoing tension.
2. **Social Issues:** Trying to fit in, handling peer conflict, or facing bullying can be a big source of stress.
3. **Family Problems:** Divorce, financial worries, or conflicts at home can make you feel uncertain or unsafe.

4. **Time Management:** Balancing school, extracurricular activities, chores, and a social life can leave you feeling like there is not enough time in the day.
5. **Future Uncertainty:** Worries about what to do after high school, or fear of not measuring up, can quietly add stress.

If you are dealing with multiple sources at once—say, tough classes plus family arguments—it can magnify your stress. In these moments, finding ways to stay calm and balanced is especially important.

---

3. Spotting Stress Signals

Each person shows stress in different ways. Here are some signs to watch for:

- **Physical Signs:** Headaches, muscle aches, upset stomach, or feeling constantly tired.
- **Emotional Signs:** Irritability, mood swings, feeling overwhelmed, or sadness.
- **Behavioral Signs:** Withdrawing from friends or activities, eating much more or less than usual, or abusing substances.
- **Cognitive Signs:** Trouble focusing, forgetting things, or constant worry.

If you notice these signs building up, it might mean stress is getting the better of you. Recognizing these signals gives you a chance to pause and decide how to handle them before they lead to deeper problems.

---

4. Organizing Your Day

One major cause of stress is feeling swamped by tasks and not knowing where to start. Creating a system to organize your day can give you a sense of control. Consider these tips:

1. **Use a Planner or App:** Jot down homework, chores, or personal tasks in a calendar. Breaking them into smaller steps can make them seem less scary.
2. **Set Priorities:** Identify which tasks are the most important and do them first. This helps you avoid last-minute panic.

3. **Plan Breaks:** Schedule short breaks between study sessions or chores. This can keep you from wearing yourself out.
4. **Be Realistic About Time:** If you know you have soccer practice until 6:00 p.m., do not plan to write a huge report the same evening. Give yourself room to breathe.

When you have a plan, it is easier to see that tasks can be done in steps. This lowers the feeling of chaos and helps you tackle one thing at a time.

5. Setting Boundaries with Commitments

Teens often feel pressure to join many clubs or be part of multiple social circles. While it is great to explore different things, overcommitting can lead to high stress. If you notice you never have time to rest or do homework, you might need to cut back. Learning to say "no" to extra activities can be tough, but it might be necessary for your mental health. You can politely tell people you have too much on your plate right now. This does not mean you will never do those activities; it just means you are choosing what is healthy for you at the moment.

6. Time Management Skills

Time management can help you lower stress by preventing rushed, last-minute work. A few approaches:

1. **Use the Two-Minute Rule:** If a task will take less than two minutes, do it right away. This can prevent small tasks from piling up.
2. **Break Down Large Tasks:** A big project can cause panic. Divide it into smaller parts—research, outline, writing, editing—and tackle each one at a time.
3. **Set Specific Goals:** Instead of saying, "I'll study tonight," say, "I'll study math for 30 minutes right after dinner, then take a break, then read English notes for 20 minutes." Clarity helps you keep track of what you are doing.
4. **Avoid Procrastination Traps:** If you know you get distracted by your phone, put it away or turn off notifications for a set time. Let friends know you will not be replying immediately. Sometimes, a short period of focused work can replace hours of half-distracted work.

With practice, good time management can free you from the stress of looming deadlines. You may even find you have more free time for activities you enjoy.

7. Relaxation Techniques

Learning techniques to calm your mind and body can be a powerful way to manage stress before it turns into anxiety or sadness. Some ideas:

1. **Progressive Muscle Relaxation:** Tense a group of muscles (like your shoulders or your fists) for a few seconds, then release. Move through different parts of your body, noticing the difference between tension and relaxation.
2. **Visualization:** Close your eyes and imagine a peaceful place—maybe the beach or a quiet forest. Picture the sights, sounds, and smells to help your mind step away from daily worries.
3. **Mindful Breathing:** Focus on each inhale and exhale. If your mind drifts, gently bring it back to your breath. Even a minute of mindful breathing can help slow a racing heart.
4. **Grounding:** Look around you and list five things you see, four things you feel, three things you hear, two things you smell, and one thing you taste. This method draws your focus to your present surroundings, quieting stressful thoughts.

Try each method at least once to see if it fits your style. Everyone reacts differently, so keep an open mind.

8. Healthy Outlets for Stress

Sometimes, you need an active way to let out stress. Here are a few outlets:

1. **Physical Activity:** Go for a jog, hit a punching bag, or follow a workout video. Moving your body can help release nervous energy and improve mood.
2. **Creative Expression:** Write a poem, draw, or even just doodle freely. You might find that expressing stress in a creative way can lessen its hold on your mind.

3. **Talking It Out:** Share your concerns with a friend, counselor, or family member. Speaking your worries aloud can help you see them more clearly and feel less alone.
4. **Playing or Listening to Music:** Music can have a powerful effect on mood. Singing along or playing an instrument can help you relax and forget about stress for a while.

If you pick an outlet you genuinely enjoy, you are more likely to stick with it. Even short sessions of these activities can help you reset.

---

9. Staying Grounded During School Hours

Stress can build quickly during the school day, especially when you move from class to class with only a few minutes in between. A few suggestions for school:

- **Use Breaks Wisely:** If you have a study hall or free period, use some of it to review notes or do light homework. Getting small tasks done can reduce your load later.
- **Eat a Balanced Lunch:** Skipping meals or having only sugary snacks can cause crashes later. Even a simple sandwich or fruit can keep you going.
- **Step Outside if Allowed:** Sometimes a quick breath of fresh air or a walk around the school courtyard can clear your mind.
- **Check in with Yourself:** During lunch, pause and see how you feel. If you are tense, try a brief relaxation technique.

By handling stress during the day, you might have more energy and a better mood by the time you get home.

---

10. Managing Social Media Stress

Social media can be fun, but it can also bring stress—seeing friends hang out without you, facing negative comments, or feeling pressured to get likes. A few ways to keep this stress in check:

1. **Limit Scrolling:** Set a time limit for social media. Constantly comparing your life to others can raise stress.

2. **Curate Your Feed:** Unfollow or mute accounts that bring you anxiety. Follow accounts that make you feel good or inform you in positive ways.
3. **Remember the Highlight Reel:** People usually post only their best moments. This can create a false impression that everyone else is always happy or successful.
4. **Stay Aware of Your Feelings:** If you notice you feel worse after browsing, log off for a bit. Your emotional well-being is more important than staying updated.

11. Building a Support System

Having trusted friends and adults in your life can ease stress by giving you people to turn to when you need to talk or get guidance. Look for those who listen without judging and offer help when you are overwhelmed. This might include family, close friends, a school counselor, or a mentor. You can also consider joining clubs or community groups where you can connect with people who share your interests. Feeling like you belong can counteract stress by reminding you that you are not alone.

12. Learning Assertive Communication

Sometimes, stress can build because you do not feel heard. Learning to speak up in a calm, honest way can help. This is called assertive communication. Instead of getting defensive or passive, say what you need clearly and politely. For example, if a friend always interrupts your study time, you could say, "I like hanging out with you, but I need time to focus on my homework. Can we plan to talk after I'm done?" This approach can prevent arguments and misunderstandings, reducing stress in your relationships.

13. Knowing Your Limits

It is okay to admit that you cannot handle everything. When you know your limits, you can decide when to ask for help or when to take a step back. For instance, if you find that juggling a job and school is affecting your sleep and mood, you might speak to your manager about cutting back hours. Or if a class is too difficult, you might meet with the teacher for extra guidance. Acknowledging limits is not weakness; it is being realistic about what you can do.

---

14. Problem-Solving for Stressful Situations

Some stress comes from problems that need solving. You can use a simple method:

1. **Identify the Problem:** For example, "I'm overwhelmed with my biology project."
2. **List Possible Solutions:** Brainstorm all ideas, even if they seem silly at first. "Work with a partner," "Ask my teacher for an extension," "Break the project into smaller tasks."
3. **Pick One and Try It:** Choose the most reasonable solution and act on it.
4. **Review the Outcome:** If it worked, great. If not, pick another solution.

This process gives you a sense of power over the situation. Instead of just worrying, you are moving toward a fix.

---

15. Physical Self-Care to Ease Stress

We talked about physical health in the previous chapter, but let us look at it from a stress angle:

- **Exercise Releases Tension:** Activities that speed up your heartbeat, like jogging or swimming, help your body burn off stress chemicals.
- **Sleep Keeps You Steady:** Without enough rest, even small hassles can feel huge. Try to keep a consistent bedtime and limit devices before bed.
- **Eating Regular Meals:** A balanced diet can keep your blood sugar levels steady, preventing mood swings that amplify stress.

Think of physical care as a shield—when your body is strong and rested, stressful events have a smaller impact on your mood.

---

16. Setting Realistic Expectations

Sometimes, stress comes from trying to reach impossible standards—either set by yourself or others. If you expect yourself to ace every single class or be liked by everyone, you are likely to feel pressured. Realistic expectations allow you to do your best without pushing yourself to the point of exhaustion. Aim for progress, not total perfection. When you catch yourself demanding perfection, ask if that expectation is fair or if it is making you feel miserable.

---

17. Humor and Stress Relief

Laughing can be a powerful stress reliever. It lowers tension, helps you breathe more deeply, and can shift your perspective. If you feel stress building up, watch a funny clip, read a humorous comic, or chat with a friend who has a good sense of humor. While humor does not solve your tasks, it can create a break from stressful thoughts and help you come back with a clearer head.

---

18. Dealing with Surprises and Changes

Life is unpredictable, and unexpected changes can cause stress. Maybe your family decides to move, or a friend suddenly changes schools. You might not be able to stop these events, but you can try to adapt:

- **Accept What You Cannot Control:** Fighting reality (like wishing the move was not happening at all) can cause added stress. Accepting that it is happening allows you to focus on what you can do next.
- **Talk About Feelings:** Share your worries or sadness with someone who listens. Sometimes just getting it out can help you manage it better.
- **Look for Small Positives:** Even in a tough situation, there might be little bright spots. For instance, if you move, you might get a bigger room or meet new friends. Noticing small positives can lessen stress.

---

19. Checking in with Yourself Daily

A useful habit is to do a quick "stress check" with yourself each day. Ask:

1. "How am I feeling right now—tense, worried, calm, sad?"
2. "What events today added to my stress?"
3. "Did I do anything helpful to handle stress?"
4. "What could I do differently next time?"

This simple reflection can help you track patterns and catch signs of too much stress early. If you see your stress climbing day after day, you can try new strategies or reach out for help before it becomes overwhelming.

20. Combining Stress Management with Professional Support

Even with good stress management, life can deliver serious challenges—a major loss, ongoing family conflict, or severe anxiety that does not go away. If stress starts to mix with constant sadness or hopelessness, it might be time to talk to a counselor or mental health professional. They can help you refine your stress management skills, explore deeper emotional issues, or suggest treatments if depression is part of the picture. Reaching out does not mean you failed at handling stress on your own; it means you recognize that extra help can lead to greater relief.

Conclusion

Stress does not have to take control of your life. By recognizing when you feel tense and using the right methods, you can keep stress at a level you can handle. Everyday actions—like planning your time, setting boundaries, trying relaxation exercises, and talking with supportive people—can make a big difference. Life will always have demands, but you have choices about how you respond.

With practice, you can develop a toolbox of stress management tactics. Over time, these actions can keep you from becoming overwhelmed and lower the chance that stress will lead you into deeper sadness or despair. Remember, you deserve to live with a mind that feels calm and capable. When stress pops up, remind yourself that you have learned ways to face it. You do not have to be perfect at it. Even small successes can encourage you to keep going. By managing stress in everyday life, you give yourself a stronger defense against depression and a healthier way to navigate the ups and downs of your teenage years.

Chapter 9: Online Pressures and Social Media

The internet can be a fun place to connect with friends, find out what is happening in the world, and learn new things. Social media platforms let you see into other people's daily lives and share parts of your own. While these connections can bring some positive benefits, there can also be challenges. Teens can feel pressured to appear perfect or stay online all the time. They might compare themselves to others, feel left out, or face mean comments. This chapter will look at how social media and the internet can affect mental health, what problems to watch out for, and how to stay emotionally safe in the online world.

1. What Makes Online Life So Appealing?

Social media gives you the ability to interact with people from all over. You can talk to someone a continent away or see pictures from a friend's party in real time. You can share your thoughts, ideas, and photos, and get reactions within seconds. This speed and reach can feel exciting. It can also give a sense of belonging when friends comment on your posts or like your pictures. For some teens, spending time online is a chance to create a space where they feel accepted, especially if their offline life is difficult.

However, the same features that make social platforms appealing can also cause problems. The constant flow of images and updates can lead to information overload. There is always something happening, so it can feel like you have to be there to keep up. This feeling can become exhausting, especially if it starts to affect your mood or self-worth.

2. The Pressure to Look Perfect

One of the most common online pressures is the belief that you must appear flawless. People often share only their happiest moments or most attractive photos. They might use filters and editing tools to smooth out skin or alter body shape. This can give the impression that everyone else is living a better life or looks better than you do. You might start to think you are the only one with flaws, messy emotions, or bad days.

This pressure can lead to a sense of insecurity. You may wonder why your life does not seem as exciting as someone else's. You could start obsessing over how you pose for a photo or whether you get enough "likes." Some teens even avoid posting pictures because they fear negative feedback. It is important to remember that much of what is posted online is curated. People usually do not show the boring, sad, or frustrating parts of their day. You see only a polished moment, not the full reality.

3. The Comparison Trap

Humans are social creatures who often look to others to measure where they stand. Online platforms make comparing yourself to others extremely easy. You may open an app and see someone else's vacation, fancy clothes, or large friend group. If you have been feeling down, it can deepen the sense that your own life is inadequate. This comparison can be harmful because it is not a fair match-up. When you compare your average day to someone's best, filtered, or staged moment, you will likely come out feeling you are missing something.

Constant comparison can lead to jealousy, low self-esteem, and sadness. You might start to believe that everyone is more successful or happier than you. However, you do not truly know what goes on behind the screen. That person with the glamorous photos might be struggling in areas you do not see. The best way to break the comparison habit is to realize you are only seeing a sliver of someone else's story. Try to focus on what is good in your own life instead of competing with an illusion.

4. Fear of Missing Out (FOMO)

FOMO refers to a strong worry that other people are having fun or living better experiences without you. Social media can make this worse because you are constantly shown updates of what your friends (or even strangers) are doing. You might see photos of a party you were not invited to or a group hanging out when you were busy. This can spark thoughts like, "Why was I left out?" or "I should be there too."

FOMO can make you anxious or push you to check apps nonstop, hoping not to miss any new update. Over time, that can lead to stress and frustration. In reality, nobody can be everywhere or do everything. Trying to keep up with every event or post is impossible. If you feel left out, it may help to plan your own hangouts or reach out directly to friends you trust. Some people find that limiting their time on social media also reduces FOMO because they are not constantly seeing posts about events they did not attend.

5. Dealing with Cyberbullying and Negative Comments

Bullying does not only happen in person. The internet can amplify harsh words because people can hide behind screens. Cyberbullying can include mean messages, spreading rumors, or sharing embarrassing photos without permission. These actions can cause a lot of emotional pain. It is also hard to get away from online bullying since social media is available 24/7, unlike bullying at school that might pause after the last bell.

If you face bullying or mean comments, try not to engage in a long back-and-forth. Save or screenshot the evidence in case you need to show an adult or administrator. Many platforms allow you to block or report users who harass you. It might feel unfair to block them if you think it admits defeat, but protecting your well-being is more important than "proving" anything to a bully. Also, do not hesitate to tell a parent, teacher, or counselor. You deserve a safe online environment.

6. The Stress of Being Always Available

Some teens feel they have to reply to texts or messages immediately, no matter what else they are doing. This can happen because of social expectations: your friends might get annoyed if you do not respond right away, or you might worry they will assume you are ignoring them. Over time, this can create a sense of pressure as you try to juggle real-life activities with the demands of online communication.

Being constantly "on call" is mentally tiring. It can interrupt your homework, your relaxation time, or moments with family. If you want to manage this stress, you can set boundaries. For example, you might decide to put your phone on silent while studying or eating dinner. If your friends complain, you can explain that you need short breaks from messaging to stay focused or to de-stress. True friends should understand that you cannot be reachable every second of the day.

7. Protecting Your Privacy

One concern that might not come up right away is online privacy. Teens sometimes share personal information, like their location or full daily schedule, without thinking about potential risks. Even if your account is private, there is a chance that screenshots or re-shares can spread your content beyond your control. Some people might not have good intentions, and you do not want to give them easy access to personal details.

It is smart to keep location settings turned off for apps that do not need them. Also, be careful about what you post or who you friend online. If you get a request from someone you do not know personally, think twice before accepting. Remember that once something is on the internet, it can be very hard to remove completely. Protecting your privacy is part of looking after your emotional health, because you avoid problems that could arise from having personal information out in public.

8. The Overload of Online Content

While social media is a big part of the online world, there are many other sources of information: news sites, blogs, video platforms, memes, and more. You can learn about almost any topic, but this can also be overwhelming. Constantly scrolling through new information can make your mind feel crowded. If you read too many tragic or frightening news stories, you may feel hopeless. If you watch hours of videos without a break, you might end up neglecting your own needs or responsibilities.

Finding balance is key. If you notice yourself feeling anxious or overloaded, step away from the screen. Go do something offline: stretch, get a snack, talk to someone in person, or take a walk. By giving your mind a break, you can come back feeling clearer and less weighed down by the flood of online content.

9. Building Healthy Online Boundaries

Many of the struggles teens face online can be eased by setting boundaries. Boundaries are like guidelines that help you decide what is and is not acceptable in your online life. They can include:

1. **Time Limits:** Decide how much time you will spend on social platforms each day. This could be 30 minutes, an hour, or any amount that fits your other responsibilities. Some phones allow you to set daily time limits for each app.
2. **Content Choices:** If certain types of accounts make you feel bad—maybe they constantly show flashy lifestyles—consider unfollowing. Fill your feed with pages that uplift or educate you in a positive way.
3. **Personal Rules for Posting:** Think about what kinds of pictures or details you are willing to share publicly. If you do not want your location known, avoid tagging yourself in real-time.
4. **Response Boundaries:** If you do not want to respond to messages at midnight, let people know you turn off your phone at a certain time. Over time, friends and family might learn to respect that you need downtime.
5. **Emotional Check-Ins:** Before you open an app, ask yourself how you feel. Are you already stressed? If so, diving into an online space might make it worse. Wait until you feel more relaxed.

By respecting these boundaries, you can keep social media in its place as a tool rather than letting it dominate your life.

10. How Social Media Affects Self-Esteem

Social media can become tied to self-esteem if you place high importance on how many likes or followers you have. You might feel proud when you get a positive response, but crushed if you do not get much attention. Over time, this can create a roller coaster of self-worth. Relying on online approval is risky because it is often based on trends, timing, and algorithms you cannot control.

Real self-esteem comes from the inside—knowing your own strengths, values, and unique traits. Remember that likes, views, or friend lists do not measure your worth. Even popular influencers face criticism and have days of low engagement. It is impossible to please everyone online. It helps to focus on creating posts or sharing content because you genuinely enjoy it, not just to gain approval.

11. Supporting Friends Online

Part of online life involves seeing your friends' posts. You might notice if someone seems sad or posts about feeling lonely. A simple comment or message can show them that you care. However, do be thoughtful. If you sense a friend might be in serious distress, encourage them to talk to a counselor or a trusted adult. If they post self-harming statements or suicidal thoughts, it is important to tell a responsible person right away—even if you worry your friend will be upset at you for sharing.

It can also help to maintain a balance between online support and in-person contact. If possible, meet up face-to-face, talk on the phone, or spend time together. Real-life interactions can provide a deeper connection than just posting comments or emojis.

12. Spotting Unrealistic Influences

Not all online content is created to help you. Some influencers or accounts push unrealistic body ideals, extreme diets, or harmful lifestyles. They might promise that you can look a certain way if you buy their products or follow their strict rules. This can harm your self-image if you start to believe you must match those standards to be attractive or successful.

It is wise to view these accounts with a critical eye. Keep in mind that influencers often earn money by promoting products. Their photos may be heavily edited. If their advice sounds too good to be true, it might not be trustworthy. If you notice yourself feeling worse after seeing a certain account, that is a sign you should stop following it. Choose content that promotes balanced information rather than impossible ideals.

13. Positive Uses of the Internet

While this chapter focuses on online pressures, remember that the internet can also be a place of growth and opportunities. You can join communities based on shared interests, such as art, music, or gaming. You can learn new skills through tutorials or free classes. You can find support groups for mental health where people share encouragement and ideas for coping.

Using the internet in ways that enrich your life can counterbalance negative aspects. If you love drawing, you can post your sketches and get constructive feedback from other artists. If you are curious about science, you can watch educational videos and even message experts. The key is to stay in control of how you use the internet, focusing on resources that build you up instead of tear you down.

---

14. Staying Safe from Strangers Online

Teens sometimes connect with strangers who have mutual interests. While many people are friendly, not everyone is. Some strangers might pretend to be someone your age, but are not who they claim to be. They could ask for personal details or try to meet in person. Always be cautious. Never share private information like your address, phone number, or full name unless you are absolutely sure who you are talking to. If someone pressures you or makes you feel uncomfortable, block them and talk to a parent or trusted adult.

Staying safe online involves common sense and listening to your instincts. If a conversation feels odd, or if a stranger quickly turns the topic to personal questions, that is a red flag. Trust your gut. You are not obligated to talk to or please someone you do not know.

---

15. Balancing Online and Offline Life

A major challenge for many teens is balancing the time spent online with time spent in real-world activities. Scrolling social media can eat up hours, leaving less time for homework, hobbies, or face-to-face relationships. Overuse of devices can also interfere with sleep if you stay awake late or check your phone in bed. Balancing means deciding how often you want to be online and then sticking to that plan as best you can.

One idea is to schedule device-free blocks of time. You might say, "After 9 p.m., I put my phone in another room" or "When I do homework, I keep my phone off unless I need it for research." Making these decisions clear to yourself and others can help you avoid aimless scrolling.

16. Handling Online Rumors or Drama

Teens sometimes face drama online—people spreading untrue gossip or stoking arguments in public posts. This can be hurtful and can damage friendships. If you find yourself caught in online drama, think about whether it is worth responding. If rumors are false, you can clarify the truth in a calm way, but avoid long fights that feed the fire. Large group chats can escalate quickly because it is easy to type heated words without seeing the other person's facial expression.

If you are upset, consider taking a break before you reply. A short pause can help you gather your thoughts and avoid saying something you might regret. If the drama is serious, involving threats or hateful language, save proof and show a teacher, counselor, or parent. It might feel embarrassing, but dealing with it early can prevent bigger problems later.

17. How Parents Can Help

You might feel annoyed at the idea of parents monitoring your online time or wanting to friend you on social platforms. Still, a caring parent can help you spot harmful trends and keep you safe. They might set rules about internet use or ask you to share if you see inappropriate content. While it can feel like an invasion of privacy, remember that many parents worry about online dangers because they have seen or heard stories where teens got hurt.

The best arrangement is an open conversation. If your parent is worried about a particular app, talk about what you actually do on it. Show them your typical feed or how you interact with friends. You can negotiate certain levels of freedom if you prove you can handle them responsibly. It is not always an easy balance to find, but working with parents rather than against them can lead to a healthier online experience.

18. Learning to Switch Off

Sometimes, the best solution for online pressure is to switch off for a while. That might mean logging out of all apps for a weekend or even turning your phone off for a few hours each day. This is not meant to punish yourself, but to help your mind reset. You may be surprised at how free you feel when you do not have to check notifications or think about what is happening on social media.

If you find yourself anxious about missing updates, remind yourself that anything truly important will still be there later. People who need to reach you for urgent reasons can call or text. A short break from the online world can help you refocus on offline interests and relationships. You might find yourself less stressed, more creative, or more in tune with how you actually feel.

19. Building Self-Confidence Outside Social Media

To stand strong against online pressures, it helps to have a sense of worth that does not rely on internet feedback. This means finding activities and personal values that matter to you outside the screen. It could be playing a sport, learning an instrument, volunteering, or simply enjoying hobbies like drawing or cooking. When you invest in these offline areas, you gain skills and confidence that remind you of who you are beyond the digital realm.

Strong self-confidence also makes it easier to handle negative comments or fewer "likes" on a post. You will remember that your value is not determined by online reactions. Instead, it is shaped by your personal qualities and actions, such as kindness, curiosity, or creativity.

Chapter 10: Handling School Challenges

School can be a place of learning, friendship, and growth, but it can also bring stress, confusion, and even anxiety. You might feel pressure to get certain grades, manage a busy schedule, or handle conflicts with teachers and classmates. For many teens, these school-related problems add to sadness or hopelessness if left unchecked. This chapter explores different types of school challenges and suggests ways to face them in a healthier way, so you can feel more confident and less overwhelmed.

1. Common Academic Pressures

One of the biggest parts of school is academics: tests, projects, homework, and grades. You might feel judged by how well you do on an exam or how quickly you can grasp a new topic. Some common issues teens face in this area include:

- **Heavy Workload:** Long reading assignments, multiple projects due at once, and constant tests can stack up quickly.
- **Difficulty in Specific Subjects:** Math, science, writing, or foreign languages can pose unique hurdles if you do not grasp the material right away.
- **Performance Anxiety:** You may fear disappointing your parents or teachers if you do not achieve high scores. Some teens even worry about their entire future if one test goes badly.
- **Lack of Motivation:** Feeling burned out or uninterested in subjects can make it tough to start assignments.

All these pressures can cause stress, which can worsen if you try to keep it all inside without seeking help.

2. Time Management at School

School days can be busy, and it is not just about going to class. You might have homework, after-school activities, part-time work, or family tasks. Handling all of these requires planning. If you struggle with time management, you might end up staying up late to finish work, which can hurt your mental health. Or you might rush through assignments and feel disappointed with the results.

To manage time better, try to plan your week with a calendar or an app. Write down deadlines, exam dates, and any extracurricular events. Break major projects into smaller parts, so you do not leave everything until the night before. Also, identify any periods you tend to waste. For instance, if you have a study hall at school, use some of that time to do homework or review notes. This approach can free up time later in the evening for rest or fun activities.

3. Facing Difficulty in Specific Subjects

It is normal not to excel in every subject. Some teens love English but struggle with math, while others find foreign languages tricky. The important thing is how you handle these struggles. If you keep quiet about your confusion, you might fall further behind and become even more stressed. Instead, consider these steps:

1. **Ask Questions in Class:** Teachers are there to guide you. If you do not understand something, try raising your hand or speaking with the teacher after class.
2. **Get Extra Help:** Many schools offer tutoring or study sessions. Some might pair you with a peer who understands the topic well.
3. **Use Online Resources:** There are plenty of free tutorials and explanations available. However, make sure you use credible sources that align with your class material.
4. **Talk to Classmates:** Forming a small study group can help you see the subject from different angles. Sometimes, a friend's explanation might make more sense than the teacher's.

If you still feel stuck, do not give up. Keep trying different methods until the topic becomes clearer. Working slowly but steadily can be more effective than trying to cram everything right before a test.

4. Handling Test Anxiety

Before a big exam, it is common to feel a rush of nerves. A bit of anxiety can sharpen your focus, but too much can block your ability to think clearly. You might blank out when you see the first question or have a racing heart the night before. Here are some ways to lessen test anxiety:

- **Prepare Gradually:** Study a bit each day rather than cramming the night before. This makes the material more familiar.
- **Practice Under Similar Conditions:** If possible, do practice questions in a quiet spot at home, timing yourself as if you were in the actual test environment.
- **Use Relaxation Techniques:** Deep breathing, positive self-talk, or a quick stretch before the test can calm your body.
- **Arrive Early:** Rushing into the classroom at the last minute can add stress. Arrive a little before the test so you can settle in and organize your thoughts.
- **Check In with Yourself:** If you feel panic rising during the test, take a few slow breaths. Remind yourself that you have studied and you can only do your best.

Even if you do not get the result you hoped for, you can learn from the experience. Talk to the teacher to see where you went wrong. This can guide you to better methods for the next exam.

---

5. Working on Group Projects

Group projects can be both helpful and frustrating. Sometimes, you get to share tasks, learn from each other, and produce a stronger final piece. But group work can also create stress if team members do not do their part or if one person tries to control everything. A few tips for smoother teamwork:

1. **Set Clear Roles:** Decide who is responsible for which part. That way, everyone knows what to do, and it is easier to hold each other accountable.

2. **Communicate Openly:** Share contact details, discuss deadlines, and check in regularly. If a problem arises, address it calmly rather than blaming anyone.
3. **Plan Early:** Do not wait until two days before the project is due. Start planning as soon as it is assigned, and schedule time to meet or communicate online.
4. **Be Flexible:** Sometimes, group members have different strengths. Let each person handle the part they are best at, but also be open to learning something new.
5. **Resolve Conflicts Kindly:** If disagreements come up, listen to each other's points of view. Try to find a solution that benefits the project rather than thinking about personal pride.

Working well in a group is a valuable skill. Even if it feels irritating at times, being able to collaborate and handle conflict can help you in future situations, whether in college or a job.

---

6. Challenging School Environments

Some schools have large class sizes, limited resources, or a harsh atmosphere. You might be in an environment where you do not feel supported or where violence and conflict are common. It is tough to concentrate on learning if you feel unsafe or disrespected. If you face such challenges, try these suggestions:

- **Seek Support from a Trusted Adult:** This could be a teacher, counselor, or coach who can advocate for you or give advice on how to handle your concerns.
- **Join Groups or Clubs:** Getting involved in a positive group can help you find friends who share your interests. It can also keep you away from negative influences.
- **Document Problems:** If you see unfair treatment, bullying, or other serious issues, note down dates and details. This can be useful if you decide to report it.
- **Look into Other Options:** In some cases, there might be alternative programs, charter schools, or online classes that fit your needs better. Talk to a counselor or parent to explore these possibilities.

Your learning environment plays a big role in your well-being. While you might not be able to change everything about it, finding small ways to create or join a positive space can reduce stress and keep you focused on your goals.

7. Dealing with Teacher Conflicts

Most teachers want to help you learn, but personalities can clash. Maybe you do not like a teacher's style, or you feel they are unfair. If this friction grows, it can affect your mood and your performance in that class. To handle teacher conflicts:

1. **Stay Respectful:** Even if you are upset, avoid rude remarks or behaviors. Disrespect usually makes problems worse.
2. **Ask for Clarification:** If you do not understand why you received a certain grade or if you disagree with feedback, calmly ask the teacher to explain. Sometimes, a talk can clear up misunderstandings.
3. **Request Extra Help:** If you are struggling, see if the teacher can suggest study tips or let you fix mistakes. Showing you want to improve can soften tensions.
4. **Find Common Ground:** Maybe the teacher has a passion for a topic or an activity you also like. Looking for that link can improve your rapport.
5. **Seek Mediation If Needed:** If you feel a teacher is truly being unfair or biased, talk to a counselor or administrator. They can guide you on the next steps.

While it is possible not every teacher-student relationship will become friendly, aiming for mutual respect can make the class less stressful. In many cases, a calm conversation is all that is needed to improve things.

8. Peer Pressure and Classmates

Teens often feel peer pressure at school. This might involve classmates pushing you to skip class, gossip, cheat on a test, or change how you dress to fit in. Giving in to peer pressure can lead to conflicts with your values or trouble with school rules. On the other hand, standing up for yourself can be tough if you worry about fitting in.

- **Know Your Values:** If you have a clear sense of what is right or wrong for you, it is easier to resist pressure.
- **Plan Your Response:** If you suspect you might be asked to do something against your comfort level, decide ahead of time what you will say.
- **Find Like-Minded Friends:** Look for people who respect your choices. True friends will not push you into doing things that make you uneasy.
- **Talk to an Adult:** If a certain group is making you feel unsafe or worried, tell a counselor, teacher, or parent.

Peer pressure can be powerful, but you have the right to stand up for yourself. If you make a choice that goes against what others say and they turn on you, they might not have been real friends in the first place.

---

9. Balancing Extracurricular Activities

Sports teams, music groups, or student organizations can be wonderful ways to explore interests and make friends. However, they also demand time and energy. If you find yourself juggling multiple after-school activities, you might end up rushing from one thing to another with little time to study or rest.

To balance these activities:

1. **Pick Quality Over Quantity:** Focus on the clubs or teams you truly enjoy or those that align with your goals. Avoid joining everything just to fill your schedule.
2. **Plan Carefully:** Mark your practices or meetings on a calendar along with school deadlines. This helps you see if your workload is manageable.
3. **Communicate with Coaches or Leaders:** If you have a big test coming up, let them know in advance. They might excuse you from a practice or allow a modified schedule.
4. **Watch for Signs of Burnout:** Feeling constantly tired, irritable, or unable to focus could mean you are doing too much. Reducing one activity can sometimes relieve a lot of stress.

Extracurriculars can add fun and depth to school life. The key is making sure they do not overload your schedule to the point that it harms your health or academics.

10. Navigating Friendships at School

Friendships at school can provide emotional support and create good memories. But they can also come with drama, misunderstandings, and changing social circles. You might grow apart from old friends or face conflicts over gossip. A few thoughts on keeping friendships healthy:

- **Communication:** If a friend does something that hurts you, speak to them directly instead of ignoring the problem. Let them know how you feel in a calm way.
- **Respect Boundaries:** Understand that friends may have different interests or might need time alone. Do not take it personally if they cannot always be there.
- **Avoid Toxic Friendships:** If a friend constantly belittles you, pressures you, or makes you feel bad about yourself, consider distancing yourself. You deserve to be treated with kindness.
- **Accept Changes:** Sometimes, people grow in different directions. That does not mean you failed as friends. It is part of life, and it can open space for new connections.

Staying open and honest can help you maintain quality friendships. Having a supportive circle can significantly ease school stress, as you can share problems and celebrate each other's successes.

---

11. Handling Rumors and Social Conflict

School hallways can be breeding grounds for rumors. Someone might say something false or spread secrets. This can be very hurtful and might isolate you. If you face rumors:

- **Confront Gently:** You can try to correct misinformation by saying, "I heard you've been saying this. It's not true. Where did you get that idea?"
- **Avoid Big Scenes:** Shouting or aggressive behavior might stir more drama.
- **Involve a Mediator:** A counselor or teacher can sometimes help resolve misunderstandings.
- **Stay True to Yourself:** If people insist on believing the rumor, focus on those who know you well and trust you.

Social conflict can also happen if different cliques or friend groups do not get along. The best approach is to keep your own actions respectful, even if others are negative.

12. The Challenge of Changing Schools

If your family moves or you transfer schools, you may feel stress about adjusting to a new environment. You might worry about not knowing anyone, getting lost in the building, or understanding the new rules. While it can feel scary, there are steps to ease the transition:

1. **Attend Orientation:** If the school offers an orientation or tour, make use of it. Knowing your way around can reduce first-day nerves.
2. **Join Clubs or Teams:** This is a quick way to meet people who share your interests.
3. **Speak with a Counselor:** They might help you select classes that fit your level and introduce you to students who can show you around.
4. **Take It One Day at a Time:** Focus on learning basic routines first—where to eat lunch, how to find your classes, who to ask for help. Over time, friendships and comfort will grow.

Everyone has been "new" at some point, so many students might be friendlier than you expect. Do not be afraid to say hi and ask basic questions. Most teens understand the awkwardness of being new.

13. Balancing School with Family Duties

Some teens have responsibilities at home, such as caring for younger siblings, cooking meals, or helping with a family business. This can make it hard to complete homework or participate in after-school events. If you are in this situation:

- **Communicate with Teachers:** Let them know you have extra duties. They might give you more flexible deadlines or suggest ways to handle your workload.

- **Ask for Help from Family Members:** If an older sibling or relative can share some chores, it might free up time for you to study.
- **Stay Organized:** Plan your household tasks alongside your school tasks. Knowing your schedule can help you see where small study pockets fit.
- **Seek Community Resources:** In some areas, community centers offer after-school tutoring or free meals, which might reduce your chores at home.

It is not always easy to balance these demands, but being open about your situation can lead to understanding and adjustments from those around you.

---

14. Keeping Up Motivation

Even if you do not face a big crisis, you might lose motivation for school. You might think, "What is the point of learning this?" or feel bored by daily routines. Low motivation can lead to missed assignments and a drop in grades, which might cause more stress later. Some ways to stay motivated:

- **Set Small Goals:** Instead of aiming for perfect grades in everything, focus on raising your next math test by one letter grade or finishing your research paper one day early.
- **Celebrate Small Wins:** If you do better on a quiz than before, give yourself credit. If you finish homework early, take a short break to do something enjoyable.
- **Relate Class Material to Real Life:** If possible, find ways the topic connects to your interests or future plans.
- **Rotate Tasks:** If you have multiple assignments, switch between subjects to keep your mind fresh.

Remember, school is about building skills for the future, not just collecting grades. Even subjects that seem pointless now might teach you how to think, research, or communicate effectively, which matters later in life.

---

15. Planning for Life After High School

Some teens feel pressured to figure out their entire future while still in school. The talk about college, jobs, or other options can be overwhelming. You might feel stressed about picking the "right" path. While it is wise to think ahead, try not to panic if you are uncertain. Consider:

- **Career Exploration:** Look into fields that interest you. Talk to people in those jobs if possible, or check out free online videos about various careers.
- **Guidance Counselors:** They can give suggestions about college or vocational training, financial aid, and scholarships.
- **Internships or Shadowing:** Spending a day or a few weeks experiencing a profession can clarify if it suits you.
- **Acceptance of Change:** Many people switch paths multiple times. Your first choice does not have to be forever.

Taking small steps to explore options can reduce anxiety. Rather than feeling locked into one choice, see it as a process of learning what suits you best.

---

16. When School Triggers Anxiety or Depression

In some cases, school itself can trigger deeper emotional issues, especially if past bullying, learning struggles, or social anxieties persist. Signs might include feeling dread each morning, having panic attacks, or thinking about skipping school entirely. If this describes you:

- **Tell a Trusted Adult:** Explain how you feel to a parent, counselor, or teacher. They cannot help unless they know how severe it is.
- **Seek Professional Support:** A therapist can help you develop coping strategies for anxiety or sadness related to school.
- **Look into 504 Plans or IEPs:** If anxiety or other conditions affect your learning, you might qualify for accommodations, like extra test time or a quieter environment.
- **Explore Alternatives:** Some teens find that home-based or online schooling helps them handle severe anxiety. Talk to your family about this if normal school is too overwhelming.

It is not weak to admit school is harming your mental health. With the right adjustments, many teens find relief and eventually return to a more balanced daily routine.

17. Finding Positive Adult Mentors

Aside from your parents, there may be other adults at school who can guide you, such as teachers, counselors, librarians, or coaches. Building a good relationship with a mentor can offer extra support, especially if you do not get it at home. These adults have more life experience and may have faced similar issues. They can provide career advice, emotional support, or simply a listening ear. Having a mentor can make you feel less alone in the school environment.

---

18. Keeping a Healthy Routine During Busy Periods

During certain times—like exam weeks or when a big project is due—you might be busier than normal. It is easy to neglect sleep, meals, or exercise. Ironically, ignoring these basic needs can make you less efficient at studying. Try to keep up a basic routine of sleep, movement, and good nutrition, even if it is harder to fit in:

- **Sleep:** Aim for at least seven to eight hours. If you have to pull a late night occasionally, try to make it the exception, not the rule.
- **Snacks and Meals:** Keep healthy snacks on hand so you do not rely on only sugary treats. A balanced meal can keep your mind sharper.
- **Movement Breaks:** Even a brief stretch or walk can wake up your brain if you have been sitting for hours.
- **Hydration:** Dehydration can make you feel tired or dizzy, so remember to drink enough water.

These small habits can give you the energy and clear head you need to tackle major school tasks without burning out.

---

19. Talking About School Issues with Family

Sometimes, teens avoid talking to parents about school problems because they fear judgment or anger. But having an open conversation can be the first step to getting help. Approach the talk calmly, maybe at a time when your parent or guardian is relaxed. Start with statements like, "I've been feeling stressed about my classes, and I'd like your input," or "I need help with a situation at school." By framing it as seeking advice instead of complaining, you might get a more supportive response.

If a parent reacts negatively at first, give them time. They might be dealing with their own stress and may not respond ideally right away. If you do not have a supportive home environment, confide in a counselor or another relative you trust. Sharing what you are going through with at least one caring adult can ease the feeling that you have to handle everything alone.

20. Learning to See School as Part of a Bigger Picture

It is easy to get wrapped up in daily school worries—quizzes, friend drama, strict teachers. But keep in mind that school is only one piece of your life. It is a place to learn important skills, meet people, and discover new interests, but it does not define your entire identity. If you do poorly on a test or fall out with a classmate, that does not decide your future. You can still grow, adapt, and find new paths.

Try to see school challenges as stepping stones for life skills. Handling a tough subject teaches persistence. Resolving conflict with a teacher teaches communication. Balancing activities trains you in planning and self-discipline. By viewing each problem as a chance to develop, you can reduce some of the fear and hopelessness that come with school stress. If you are patient with yourself and ask for help when needed, you may find that school becomes more manageable and even a source of pride, rather than a constant obstacle.

Conclusion

School can bring heavy demands that affect your mood and sense of worth. From deadlines and exams to teacher conflicts and peer pressure, there are many hurdles that might leave you feeling overwhelmed. Remember, you do not have to face these alone. By learning to organize your schedule, seek help when you are stuck, communicate with teachers or classmates in a respectful way, and maintain a healthy routine, you can reduce much of the stress tied to school.

Chapter 11: Friends and Peer Influence

Having friends is an important part of being a teen. Friends can make you laugh, help you explore new interests, and give you a sense of belonging. At the same time, friendships can be challenging. Conflicts might arise, or you might feel pressured to do things that do not align with your values. Peer influence can shape your choices in both positive and negative ways. This chapter will explore how friends and peers impact your mood and well-being, plus ways to keep friendships healthy and supportive.

---

1. The Importance of Friends in Teen Life

During your teen years, you are often trying to figure out who you are. Friends can be part of this process by exposing you to new experiences or showing you different outlooks. A good friend provides companionship, emotional support, and a chance to grow socially.

- **Shared Activities:** Whether you enjoy gaming, playing sports, or discussing books, friends give you someone to enjoy these pastimes with. This can help you feel less isolated.
- **Understanding and Empathy:** Friends around your age might understand your daily concerns, from school stress to feeling unsure about the future. Knowing you are not alone can reduce worry.
- **Practical Help:** In some cases, friends help you with homework, give you rides, or share advice about classes or part-time jobs.

When friendships are positive, they can act as a cushion against sadness. If you have a bad day, talking it through with a trusted friend might help you feel better. However, when friendships are stormy or involve harmful behaviors, they can make feelings of depression worse. It is important to recognize which friendships are helpful and which are harmful.

---

2. Understanding Peer Influence

Peer influence occurs when the people around your age affect your actions or thoughts. This can happen in many ways:

- **Direct Pressure:** When someone urges you to do something, like try a cigarette or skip class.
- **Indirect Pressure:** When you notice your friends dressing a certain way or listening to a certain type of music, and you feel compelled to do the same to fit in.
- **Emotional Influence:** When your friends' moods and beliefs rub off on you. For example, if a close friend is very negative, you might start to see life more darkly, too.

Peer influence is not always bad. It can motivate you to join a club, study harder, or volunteer if your group values those things. The key is learning to tell when influence is helping you grow versus dragging you into risky or negative behaviors.

---

3. Identifying Positive Friendships

A positive friendship usually leaves you feeling good about yourself and hopeful about life. Here are some markers of a healthy friendship:

1. **Mutual Respect:** You and your friend respect each other's boundaries, opinions, and feelings. There is no belittling or shaming.
2. **Trust:** You can share personal things without fearing they will spread the information or mock you.
3. **Honesty and Support:** When you succeed at something, a good friend is genuinely happy for you. When you struggle, they are willing to listen or help if they can.
4. **Balance:** Both of you contribute to the relationship. One person does not consistently give all the emotional support while the other person only receives.
5. **Freedom to Be Yourself:** You do not have to pretend to be someone else. You can share your real interests, sense of humor, or taste in music without feeling judged.

When these elements are present, friendships often boost your self-esteem and help you cope with life's challenges. Positive friends do not have to be perfect—everyone has flaws—but they should make you feel valued rather than torn down.

4. Recognizing Harmful or Toxic Friendships

Sometimes, a friend might behave in ways that harm your well-being. These friendships can worsen depression or stress. Signs of a potentially harmful friendship include:

1. **Constant Criticism or Bullying:** You feel belittled or mocked often, even if they say "It's just a joke."
2. **Control and Manipulation:** A friend might push you to do things you are not comfortable with or threaten to end the friendship if you do not comply.
3. **Lack of Empathy:** They ignore or dismiss your feelings, making you feel unheard or small.
4. **Jealousy and Possessiveness:** They do not want you to have other friends or hobbies, and you always have to put them first.
5. **Frequent Conflict with No Resolution:** Arguments happen all the time, but there is no attempt to solve the problems or show understanding.

Being stuck in a harmful friendship can leave you drained, anxious, or down on yourself. You might feel better once you step back or limit your contact with that person. In some cases, you can address the issues by communicating and setting boundaries. If nothing improves, it may be wise to distance yourself or end the friendship for the sake of your mental health.

---

5. How Friends Affect Mood and Self-Image

Friends can influence the way you see yourself. If friends tease you about your appearance or abilities, you might start to believe those criticisms. On the other hand, supportive friends can help you build confidence. When you share achievements with a friend who celebrates them, you feel proud. When a friend notices you are acting down and checks on you, it can lessen loneliness.

If you notice that spending time with certain friends leaves you feeling anxious or ashamed, it may be time to evaluate what is happening. Do you feel pressured to hide parts of your personality? Do they often focus on your flaws? Sometimes, reflecting on these questions can clarify whether a friendship is beneficial or not.

6. Dealing with Peer Pressure

Peer pressure can be tricky because you might worry about losing friends if you do not go along with them. But giving in to pressure that leads to harmful activities—like underage drinking, drug use, or bullying someone—can have long-lasting consequences.

- **Set Clear Boundaries:** Know in advance what you are not willing to do. That might mean deciding, "I will not try smoking," or "I will not ditch class."
- **Practice Firm Responses:** You can prepare a polite but firm phrase, such as "No, I'm not comfortable with that," or "Sorry, that's not my thing."
- **Suggest Alternatives:** If friends want to do something risky, propose a safer or healthier activity. This shows you are not rejecting them, just the behavior.
- **Find Allies:** If at least one other person in the group also feels uneasy, it is easier to resist pressure together.
- **Be Willing to Walk Away:** If people refuse to respect your stance, it might be necessary to remove yourself from the situation or the group.

Standing up to peer pressure can be scary, but it strengthens your self-respect. Over time, you may attract friends who appreciate you for who you are, rather than pressuring you to do things that feel wrong.

---

7. Making New Friends

If you feel lonely or sense that your current group of friends is not supportive, you might consider meeting new people. This can be daunting, especially if you are shy. Here are some ideas:

1. **Join Clubs or Groups:** Look for student clubs, hobby groups, or volunteer organizations. Shared interests make it easier to strike up conversations.
2. **Start Small Talk:** Say hello to someone who sits near you in class or who has the same study hall. You can ask about a shared subject or an upcoming school event.
3. **Use Your Interests:** If you like art, you could sign up for an art workshop. If you enjoy gaming, you could find a local or online gaming group.

4. **Offer Help:** If you notice someone struggling in a subject you are good at, offer to study together. This can lead to friendship.
5. **Be Open and Kind:** A smile, a friendly greeting, or a compliment about someone's T-shirt can break the ice.

Remember that forming closer friendships often takes time. If you do not form strong bonds right away, keep being kind and approachable. You never know which small interaction could lead to a new friend.

---

8. Strengthening Current Friendships

You might already have a few good friends, but perhaps you want to grow closer or deepen those connections. Friendship is not just about hanging out; it involves trust, honest communication, and understanding. Here are some ways to make your existing friendships stronger:

1. **Be a Good Listener:** When your friend is sharing a concern, put away distractions and give them your attention. Ask follow-up questions instead of rushing to talk about yourself.
2. **Show Genuine Interest:** Ask about their passions or their day. Even a short text asking, "How are you doing?" can show you care.
3. **Offer Support:** If your friend is stressed about a test or going through a hard time, see if there is something you can do. This might mean studying together or just being there to listen.
4. **Respect Their Space:** Even best friends need time alone or with other people. Avoid taking it personally if they want some time apart.
5. **Address Problems Early:** If you notice tension, bring it up calmly. Try statements like, "I've sensed we're not talking as much. Is something bothering you?" Clearing misunderstandings early can prevent bigger conflicts.

---

9. Communicating About Feelings and Boundaries

Friends are not mind readers. They do not always know when you feel uncomfortable, hurt, or in need of help. That is why clear communication matters:

- **Express Emotions:** If your friend's joke hurt your feelings, let them know in a calm way: "That joke made me feel bad. I'd prefer if you didn't make fun of that."
- **Voice Your Limits:** If you need time for homework or personal space, you can say, "I'd love to hang out, but I have a project due tomorrow. Maybe we can meet up this weekend?"
- **Encourage Them to Speak:** Ask them how they are feeling, and be prepared to listen without judging. This can deepen trust on both sides.

Many friendship conflicts happen because people assume the other person already knows something. By speaking openly about your feelings, you keep misunderstandings to a minimum and create a safer bond.

---

10. Friendship Breakups and Changing Circles

Not all friendships last forever. You might find that you outgrow certain relationships or that someone's behavior becomes too harmful to tolerate. Ending a friendship or distancing yourself is not easy, but it can be necessary:

- **Evaluate the Issues:** Is the conflict a misunderstanding that can be fixed, or do you see no sign of positive change?
- **Communicate Clearly:** If you decide to end a friendship, you can say something like, "I need some space. I appreciate our time together, but I feel we are going in different directions right now."
- **Be Respectful:** You do not have to insult or attack them. Simply state your stance.
- **Grieve the Loss:** A friendship breakup can be painful. It is normal to feel sad or even guilty. Give yourself time to process these emotions.
- **Seek Support Elsewhere:** Lean on family, a counselor, or other friends to help you move forward.

As painful as it can be, letting go of a toxic friendship can free you from negative cycles. You can then focus on healthier connections that contribute to your well-being.

---

11. When a Friend Struggles with Depression

You might notice a friend showing signs of depression—sadness, withdrawal, or hopelessness. This can be alarming, and you might not know how to help. Some steps you can take:

1. **Listen with Compassion:** Let them talk about what they are experiencing. You can say, "I'm here for you. It's okay to feel this way." Avoid judging or offering quick fixes like, "Just cheer up."
2. **Encourage Professional Help:** If they seem overwhelmed or talk about harmful thoughts, encourage them to see a counselor, speak to a parent, or reach out to a helpline. You can offer to accompany them if they feel nervous.
3. **Check In Regularly:** A simple text or call asking how they are doing can remind them they are not alone.
4. **Do Not Take on the Role of Therapist:** You can be supportive, but you are not a trained counselor. If your friend's situation is serious, they need professional care.
5. **Talk to a Trusted Adult if Needed:** If your friend mentions harmful thoughts or actions, do not keep it a secret. It might feel like a betrayal, but your friend's safety matters most.

Supporting a friend with depression can be emotionally draining. Be sure to look after your own mental health, too. You cannot pour from an empty cup.

---

12. Handling Friendship Conflicts and Fights

Fights can happen in even the best friendships, often due to misunderstandings, jealousy, or hurt feelings. A few strategies for handling conflict:

- **Stay Calm:** If you are upset, take a moment to breathe before responding. Anger can cause you to say things you regret.
- **Use "I" Statements:** Blaming the other person can escalate the problem. Instead, say, "I felt left out when you didn't invite me." This focuses on your feelings rather than attacking them.
- **Hear Their Side:** Let your friend explain how they see the issue. Sometimes, understanding their perspective can soften your stance.

- **Look for Compromise:** Maybe both of you can adjust a little to meet in the middle. It is rarely a matter of one person being totally right and the other being totally wrong.
- **Apologize if Needed:** If you realize you were at fault, a sincere apology can heal wounds. Saying, "I'm sorry for how I reacted" can mean a lot.

If the conflict remains unresolved and causes ongoing stress, you might seek help from a counselor or a mediator. Some schools have peer mediation programs where a neutral party helps students talk out their disagreements.

---

13. Balancing Friendships with Other Parts of Life

Sometimes, friendships can become so central that you let other parts of your life slide—like schoolwork, family time, or personal hobbies. It is natural to enjoy time with friends, but having a balanced life is also important. You can:

- **Create a Schedule:** Mark times for homework, family dinners, and relaxation. Fit in social activities around those.
- **Say "No" to Some Plans:** If a friend wants to hang out every single afternoon, but you need time to study or recharge, politely decline sometimes.
- **Keep Hobbies and Goals in Sight:** If you abandon your own interests just to follow a friend's interests, you may feel unfulfilled. A healthy friendship allows each person to retain their individuality.

Setting these boundaries does not mean you value your friend any less; it shows you also value your personal growth and well-being. Friends who truly care about you will respect that you have multiple priorities.

---

14. Online Friendships and Peer Influence

In today's world, many teen friendships happen or begin online. You might connect through social media, gaming platforms, or shared interest groups. While online friends can be supportive, there are a few special considerations:

1. **Safety Concerns:** Make sure you know who you are talking to. Never share personal details like your full address or bank information.
2. **Online Personas vs. Reality:** People can portray themselves in ways that are not entirely genuine. Be cautious about trusting someone's every word if you have never met them in person.
3. **Cyberbullying:** Online group chats can become toxic if bullying or negative comments go unchecked. Know how to block or report harmful behavior.
4. **Balancing On-Screen and Off-Screen Time:** Too much online socializing can prevent you from developing real-life interactions. Try to keep a healthy mix of both.

If an online friend starts encouraging you to do harmful things or becomes possessive, remember that you can log off, block them, or reach out to a trusted adult. Your emotional and physical safety come first.

---

15. Supporting Someone Facing Peer Pressure

It might be that a close friend is the one dealing with peer pressure. They could be torn about following a certain trend or feeling pushed to do things that make them uneasy. You can help them by:

- **Listening Without Judgment:** Let them vent about the pressure. Even if you do not fully agree, hearing them out can be a relief for them.
- **Discussing Options:** You can brainstorm safe responses or alternatives. For example, if they do not want to go to a risky party, you can suggest a different activity.
- **Practicing Role-Play:** Sometimes, trying out how to say "no" in a safe environment can build your friend's confidence.
- **Encouraging Them to Stand Firm:** Remind them that true friends will understand if they say "no." Real friendship does not require harmful actions or behaviors.

By being supportive, you might help your friend avoid a bad choice or a downward spiral. It also shows them you are someone they can rely on when they feel pressured.

16. Building Self-Confidence to Handle Peer Influence

One reason peer pressure works is that many teens want acceptance. If you do not feel secure in who you are, you may compromise your values or well-being to keep friends. Building your self-confidence can lower the power of negative influences:

- **Acknowledge Your Strengths:** Make a list of what you do well—maybe you are good at drawing, math, or comforting people. Remind yourself of these skills when doubts arise.
- **Set Personal Goals:** Having your own goals, like learning a new language or mastering a sport, can give you a sense of direction. This makes you less likely to do random things just to fit in.
- **Spend Time Alone:** A bit of solitude can help you figure out your thoughts without anyone else's input. Understanding yourself can strengthen your ability to stand by your opinions.
- **Try New Activities:** Exploring new hobbies can expand your skills and your circle of potential friends. It can also show you capabilities you did not know you had.
- **Affirmation and Positive Self-Talk:** When you feel pressured, silently remind yourself: "My worth does not depend on their approval."

Over time, you can develop a stronger sense of self. Then, peer influence—while still present—will not sway you as easily if it goes against your well-being.

---

17. Seeking Adult Help for Friendship Problems

Sometimes, friendship problems can be too overwhelming to handle alone. If a friend is involved in dangerous behavior or if you feel trapped in a negative group, speaking to an adult can be essential. Possible adults to approach:

- **School Counselor:** They have experience with teen conflicts and can offer strategies or mediate if necessary.
- **Teacher or Coach:** If they know you and your friend, they might offer understanding or step in if situations escalate, such as bullying.
- **Parent or Guardian:** They can provide advice, set boundaries, or contact the school if the issue involves harassment or safety threats.

- **Trusted Family Friend:** If you are not comfortable talking to your own parents, maybe an aunt, uncle, or older cousin can guide you.

Some teens hesitate to involve adults because they fear it will make them seem weak or because they do not want to be a "snitch." However, if the emotional strain is heavy or if serious risks exist, getting help is a sign of responsibility. Your mental health and safety matter more than maintaining an illusion of independence.

---

18. Learning from Friendship Mistakes

Everyone makes mistakes in friendships. You might have judged someone unfairly, shared a friend's secret, or acted too clingy. Rather than beat yourself up, try to learn from these slip-ups:

1. **Reflect on What Went Wrong:** Did you act out of jealousy or insecurity? Understanding the root cause can prevent the same error in the future.
2. **Apologize Sincerely:** If you hurt someone, an honest apology can help repair trust. Recognize what you did and express how you plan to do better.
3. **Set Steps to Improve:** If you have a habit of gossiping, you might decide to pause and ask, "Is this helpful or hurtful?" before speaking.
4. **Forgive Yourself:** Dwelling on guilt forever is not productive. Once you make amends, give yourself permission to move on.

Mistakes are part of growing. They teach you about who you are and how you relate to others. By applying what you learn, you become a better friend in the long run.

---

19. Cultural and Family Differences Among Friends

Some friend groups have people from different backgrounds, religions, or family structures. Learning to respect these differences can deepen friendships and broaden your perspective:

- **Be Curious, Not Judgmental:** Ask questions politely about customs or traditions you do not understand. Most people appreciate interest rather than silent confusion.
- **Respect Beliefs and Boundaries:** If a friend cannot participate in certain activities because of their beliefs, do not pressure them. Show acceptance.
- **Avoid Stereotypes:** Do not assume you know everything about someone's background. Let them define who they are.
- **Share Your Own Culture or Traditions:** This can strengthen the bond and allow for mutual understanding.

When friends honor each other's differences, it can create a deeper connection. You might learn wonderful things about foods, languages, or celebrations you never knew existed.

---

20. Finding Balance in Friendship and Personal Growth

Friendships are an ever-shifting part of teen life. People change, interests evolve, and you might not stay close with the same group from year to year. That is natural, even if it feels sad at times. Try to keep a sense of balance:

- **Nurture a Few Close Bonds:** Having many acquaintances is fine, but a small circle of trusted friends can provide more meaningful support.
- **Respect Yourself and Others:** Stand up for your boundaries and needs, but also show empathy and kindness.
- **Allow Space for Growth:** You and your friends are growing at different rates. Give them room to explore their own lives, and do the same for yourself.
- **Stay Open to New Connections:** You never know who you might click with in a future class, club, or job.

Healthy friendships can serve as a positive influence, supporting you through life's ups and downs. At the same time, you can support your friends, learning empathy, communication, and problem-solving skills. By being mindful of peer influence—both helpful and harmful—you lay a foundation for stronger self-confidence and emotional well-being.

Chapter 12: Talking with Family

Family plays a major role in many teens' lives, whether you live with both parents, a single parent, grandparents, or other relatives. Family members can be your biggest supporters. They can also be a source of conflict or stress. Learning to communicate with them in an effective way can help ease tension, prevent misunderstandings, and build stronger bonds. This chapter will look at why talking with family can be tough, how to get past typical barriers, and how to find support within your home when you are feeling down.

1. Why Family Communication Matters

Your family is often the group of people you see the most, whether at meals, during weekends, or in daily chores. They might care about you deeply, but that does not guarantee smooth communication. You may feel embarrassed about certain topics or fear that your family will judge you. Yet, talking to a family member about your worries can help you gain perspective and emotional backing. Good family communication can:

- **Reduce Loneliness:** Knowing someone at home cares about your day can help you feel less alone with your problems.
- **Provide Guidance:** Relatives who have experienced ups and downs might share insights that help you avoid pitfalls.
- **Offer Resources:** Parents or guardians can provide financial assistance for therapy or help you schedule doctor visits if needed.
- **Strengthen Bonds:** Open conversations deepen your connection. This can make home a safer, more nurturing place.

2. Common Barriers to Talking with Family

Even if you want to share your struggles, there might be roadblocks:

1. **Fear of Disapproval:** You might worry that your parents will be upset or disappointed if you tell them about bad grades, friend conflicts, or mental health concerns.

2. **Cultural or Generational Gaps:** If your family is from a culture where emotional problems are not discussed, or if your parents grew up in a very different era, they might not relate easily to your experiences.
3. **Overprotectiveness:** Some parents try to shield their teens from everything, which might lead you to hide your true thoughts to avoid strict rules.
4. **Previous Conflicts:** If you have had arguments or felt judged in the past, you might hesitate to open up again.
5. **Lack of Time:** In busy households, it can be hard to find a calm moment to sit and talk.

Acknowledging these barriers can help you find ways around them. Not every family situation is ideal, but even small improvements in communication can bring relief.

3. Deciding What to Share

Teens sometimes ask, "Do I have to tell my family everything?" The answer is usually no. You are allowed to have some privacy. However, if you struggle with deep sadness, anxiety, or any thoughts of harming yourself, letting at least one trusted family member know is important for your safety. Examples of topics you might share:

- **Major Emotional Distress:** If you are feeling hopeless or unable to cope, telling a parent or guardian can be the first step to finding professional help.
- **School Issues:** If you are overwhelmed with homework, bullied, or struggling academically, family members can advocate for you or help in practical ways.
- **Changes in Behavior:** If you have been losing sleep, eating less, or showing other signs of stress, letting them know can help them understand why you might be moody or tired.
- **Trouble with Peers:** If friends are pressuring you to do things you are uncomfortable with, discussing it can bring you clarity or support.

Try not to wait until problems become emergencies. Opening up earlier can prevent bigger issues. If you are unsure whether to share something, think about whether it affects your well-being. If it does, it is probably worth bringing up.

4. Finding the Right Time and Place

Talking about serious matters in the middle of a rushed morning or when your family is stressed might not lead to a good conversation. Choose a moment when people are more relaxed:

- **Quiet Evening:** After dinner or before bedtime can be a calmer time for conversation.
- **Weekend Afternoon:** If your family has a day off, you can ask them to sit down and talk when nobody is rushing to work or school.
- **Private Setting:** If your home is crowded, you can ask to speak in a separate room or go for a walk. You want a space where you can share freely without interruptions.
- **Ask for Their Attention:** You could say, "I have something important on my mind. Is this a good time to talk?" This heads-up can help them focus on you.

Sometimes, you might not have the luxury of a perfect moment, especially if something urgent happens. But if you can, planning ahead increases the chance of a calm, productive talk.

---

5. Getting Past Awkwardness

Discussing personal problems, mental health, or sensitive topics with family can feel weird if you are not used to it. A few ways to make it less awkward:

- **Write It Down:** If speaking face-to-face is too hard, you can start with a short letter, note, or text that says you need to talk.
- **Use "I" Statements:** Instead of saying, "You never understand me," say, "I feel misunderstood when you respond that way." This lowers the chance of the other person becoming defensive.
- **Start with a Smaller Topic:** If you have never talked about your feelings, you might begin by sharing a minor worry, like a small issue at school, to get more comfortable.
- **Admit the Awkwardness:** You can say, "I'm not used to talking about this stuff, and I feel nervous." Sometimes, being honest about feeling uncomfortable can relieve some pressure.

Remember that many parents also feel uncertain about how to start these conversations. They might not be sure how to react. Patience with each other can go a long way.

6. Explaining Your Emotions Clearly

When you say "I'm sad" or "I'm stressed," family members might not realize how serious it is. Try to use specific examples:

- **Describe the Intensity:** Instead of, "I'm sad all the time," you can say, "For the past two weeks, I wake up feeling like I can't face the day. I cry almost every night."
- **List Changes in Behavior:** Mention if you have stopped enjoying activities, lost appetite, or are struggling to sleep. Concrete details help them see the impact on your daily life.
- **Connect It to Events (If Possible):** If a recent change at home or a friendship issue triggered your sadness, mention it. For example, "I think I've felt worse since my best friend moved away."
- **Express What You Need:** If you need therapy, say, "I feel I'd benefit from talking to a professional." If you need more understanding, you could say, "I'd appreciate it if you could check in with me each day."

By painting a clear picture, you allow your family to grasp the seriousness of your feelings. This makes it easier for them to respond with genuine help.

7. Handling Negative Reactions

Even the best-prepared conversation can end with a response you did not want. A parent might react with anger, denial, or dismissiveness. This can be heartbreaking if you finally mustered the courage to open up. Here are some steps to manage that:

- **Stay Calm:** Getting defensive can escalate the conflict. Take a deep breath and try to keep your tone steady.
- **Re-Emphasize Your Feelings:** You might say, "I understand this is surprising, but I need you to know I feel this way every day."

- **Ask for Another Time to Talk:** If tensions are running high, it might help to step away and suggest talking again later when emotions have cooled.
- **Seek Alternative Support:** If your immediate family is not supportive, consider reaching out to a different relative, such as an aunt or older cousin, or talk to a school counselor.
- **Remember You Are Not at Fault:** Their reaction might stem from their own fears or stress, not from you doing something wrong.

Not every parent or guardian reacts ideally, especially if they have their own anxieties or misunderstandings about mental health. It might take multiple tries, or you might need a mediator such as a counselor, to bridge the gap.

8. Asking for Professional Help Together

In many cases, you might benefit from seeing a therapist or counselor, and having a supportive family member can make this process smoother. You could say:

- **"I'd Like to See a Counselor":** If your parent seems unsure, explain that it's to help you handle sadness or stress before it gets worse.
- **Discuss Practical Aspects:** Who will pay for it? Which counselor will you see? How will you get there? Show that you have thought these details through or are willing to figure them out together.
- **Invite Them to Family Sessions:** Some therapists offer family sessions if needed. This can help everyone learn better communication and coping strategies.

Getting professional help is not a sign of weakness. It is a proactive step that can benefit your entire household if family members cooperate.

9. Cultural or Language Barriers

In some families, parents might speak a different first language, making it hard to share deeper feelings. Or, the culture might discourage talking about personal struggles. Here are ways to address this:

- **Use a Bilingual Friend or Relative:** If language is a barrier, a trusted bilingual person might help explain your feelings accurately.
- **Seek Cultural-Sensitive Counselors:** If you decide to get therapy, look for professionals familiar with your cultural background who understand how cultural values affect emotional issues.
- **Start with Shared Values:** If your family values harmony, you can say, "I want our home to feel supportive. That's why I need to tell you how I'm really feeling."
- **Educate Gently:** If your parents do not believe in mental health issues, you might show them reliable articles in their language or share real stories of people who have improved with help.

Changing a cultural mindset does not happen overnight. Patience and gentle communication can lead to gradual understanding.

---

10. Balancing Family Needs and Personal Boundaries

In some homes, teens feel pulled in many directions—helping with siblings, chores, or family responsibilities. While contributing is part of family life, you also have personal needs:

- **Set Limits Kindly:** You can say, "I'm happy to help with chores, but I need an hour each night for homework and personal time."
- **Negotiate Responsibilities:** If you feel overwhelmed, see if tasks can be shared with siblings or if your parents can lighten your load during busy school periods.
- **Explain How Stress Affects You:** Saying, "I'm getting headaches because of too much pressure," might help them see the need to reduce demands.
- **Be Willing to Compromise:** Maybe you cannot avoid all chores, but your family might allow you to skip one or two tasks during exam weeks.

Balancing your well-being with family obligations can ease tension. It also shows you respect the household while caring for yourself.

11. When a Family Member Has Their Own Struggles

Sometimes, the person you wish to talk to is dealing with their own problems—maybe a parent has lost a job or is facing health issues. In that case:

- **Choose the Right Moment:** If they are in the middle of a crisis, it might be harder for them to give you support. Wait until they are more stable, if possible.
- **Show Empathy:** Acknowledge their stress. For example, "I know you're going through a lot, but I'm having a tough time too. Could we help each other?"
- **Suggest Outside Support:** If your family is in crisis, it might help to involve a family friend, relative, or professional who can support everyone.
- **Stay Patient:** They might not respond right away. If you do not get the help you need, seek someone else to talk to, like a school counselor.

Family members cannot always handle everything, but by showing understanding, you might build a bridge for mutual support.

---

12. Dealing with Strict or Overprotective Parents

Some parents keep very tight rules or want to monitor everything you do. This can cause friction if you feel you have no freedom or privacy. Approaching these parents about your emotional challenges might feel risky, but consider:

- **Pick a Good Time:** Talk when they are less likely to be stressed, perhaps after dinner or on a weekend morning.
- **Explain Your View Calmly:** Let them know you understand they want to keep you safe, but also share how constant oversight increases your stress.
- **Offer Solutions:** For instance, "I'll check in with you by text every hour when I'm out, but please let me go out with friends for two hours without calling me constantly."
- **Show Responsibility:** If you consistently follow agreed-upon rules, they might trust you more. For example, if you promise to be home by 8 p.m., do it. Over time, they might loosen controls.

- **Seek Mediation:** If your parents do not budge, a counselor or family therapist might help find a middle ground.

Respecting parents' concerns while standing up for your emotional needs is a delicate balance. Patience and consistent behavior can make a big difference over time.

---

13. Communicating with Siblings

Siblings can be a source of comfort or conflict. If you have a close bond with a brother or sister, they might be your first line of support. But siblings can also tease or compete with you. Tips for better sibling communication:

- **Find Shared Interests:** Even if you argue, you might both like a particular movie, game, or activity. Spending time on shared interests can strengthen your connection.
- **Ask for Help or Offer It:** If you are older, guide your younger sibling through school problems. If you are younger, you might ask for advice about classes. Mutual support can replace rivalry.
- **Set Boundaries:** Let them know if certain teasing crosses a line or if you need time alone in your room. Also, respect their boundaries.
- **Team Up for Family Issues:** If your parents are strict or a household problem arises, siblings can unite and talk to parents together. A combined voice might be taken more seriously.

Siblings know your family situation best. In a supportive relationship, they can be a strong ally. If sibling rivalry is serious, a family counselor might help you and them learn better ways to relate.

---

14. When Talking Is Not Enough

Sometimes, communication alone does not solve family problems, particularly if there is ongoing conflict, abuse, or mental health issues that affect multiple family members. In these cases:

- **Professional Counseling:** Family therapy sessions can help everyone learn better ways to handle emotions and solve arguments.
- **Speak to a Trusted Adult:** If you experience any kind of abuse, it is important to tell a counselor, teacher, or relative outside your immediate home.
- **Support Groups:** Some communities have support groups for teens dealing with specific family issues, like a parent's substance misuse or divorce.
- **Emergency Hotlines:** If you do not feel safe or have thoughts of harming yourself, reach out to a crisis helpline. It is confidential and can guide you to urgent help.

Talking is a strong starting point, but do not hesitate to look for outside resources if family issues are overwhelming or unsafe.

---

15. Small Wins in Communication

15. Acknowledging Small Signs of Progress in Communication

Improving family communication is usually a gradual process. Your parent might still be learning how to respond, or your sibling may not fully understand what you are going through. Recognize small signs of progress:

- **A Positive Response:** Maybe your mom asked how you slept. That shows an interest in your well-being.
- **A Less Heated Argument:** Even if you argued, it might have been calmer than before. That is a step toward respectful communication.
- **A Change in Rules:** If a parent allowed you more freedom after discussing your need for independence, it shows some trust is building.
- **Moments of Empathy:** If a sibling offered you comfort after a rough day, that is a sign the connection is improving.

Not every conversation will go smoothly, but these small improvements can build hope. Over time, a series of small steps can make a big difference in the household's emotional atmosphere.

---

16. Blended or Non-Traditional Families

Some teens live in blended families with stepparents, step-siblings, or half-siblings. Others live with grandparents or foster families. Communication can become more complicated when multiple households or new family members join in. If this applies to you:

- **Give Time for Adjustment:** Everyone might need time to get used to the new family dynamic. Rushing acceptance can cause tension.
- **Be Clear About Feelings:** If a stepparent tries to take on a parenting role too soon, kindly express your comfort level. A statement like, "I appreciate your concern, but can we talk about how we set rules together?" might help.
- **Share Household Responsibilities Fairly:** Blended families might disagree on chores or discipline. Clear rules that apply equally to all siblings can lower fights.
- **Find Neutral Activities:** Engage in family activities where no one feels singled out. Board games, cooking a simple meal together, or watching a neutral TV show can help people bond.
- **Seek Outside Guidance:** If conflicts remain high, a family counselor familiar with blended-family challenges can provide tailored advice.

Blended families can bring wonderful new connections, but it takes open-mindedness and respectful communication to create harmony under one roof.

---

17. Encouraging Family Members to Learn About Mental Health

If your family seems uninformed about depression or anxiety, you could encourage them to learn more:

- **Share Resources:** Offer articles or videos from trustworthy sources that explain teen depression or stress.
- **Invite Them to Ask Questions:** Let them know they can ask you or a professional if they are confused about mental health terms.

- **Open Up About Therapy:** If you are in therapy, you might share something you learned or a technique that helps you. This can show your family how therapy benefits you.
- **Remind Them It Is Common:** Point out that many people experience mental health problems. This can reduce stigma or shame.

When families learn the basics of mental health, they might become more understanding and supportive. Sometimes, they may even start to address their own emotional well-being alongside yours.

18. Respecting Differences in Opinion

You and your family members will not always agree. Parents might hold different beliefs about chores, curfews, or future plans. That does not mean you should avoid expressing yourself. Instead:

- **Agree to Disagree Sometimes:** It is possible to maintain a relationship without resolving every disagreement.
- **Look for Common Ground:** Maybe you disagree on curfew time, but you both care about safety. Understanding each other's reasons can soften the debate.
- **Keep the Tone Polite:** If you must stand your ground, do it respectfully. Hostile language can cause defensiveness, halting real communication.
- **Reflect on Their Perspective:** Sometimes parents' rules stem from concern for your safety rather than a desire to control you.

Balancing your individuality with family views is part of growing up. Learning to express disagreement kindly is a valuable skill that helps you in all relationships.

19. When Family Shows Support

If your family responds well and offers help when you open up about feeling depressed or stressed, great! You can:

- **Make a Plan Together:** Discuss whether you need therapy, a new schedule, or a doctor's visit. Having a clear plan can reduce your anxiety about what comes next.
- **Accept Their Efforts:** If they check on you or try to spend more quality time together, see these actions as signs of care.
- **Give Feedback:** If something they do is or is not helpful, let them know. For example, "I really appreciate you asking how I'm feeling every night. It makes me feel supported."
- **Include Them in Progress:** If therapy is part of your plan, you might share updates like, "I learned a new coping skill this week," so they see how their support matters.

A caring family can make a big difference in dealing with low mood or daily stress. Their involvement can boost your motivation to keep trying healthy strategies.

---

20. Moving Forward with Healthy Family Communication

Teen years are a period of many shifts. Families, too, are constantly adapting. By learning to speak openly with your parents, siblings, or guardians, you lay the groundwork for a healthier emotional environment. Even if some family members do not respond perfectly, each honest effort can bring you closer to understanding one another.

- **Stay Patient:** Change within a family often happens slowly.
- **Be Brave in Sharing Feelings:** Your emotions are valid, and you deserve to be heard.
- **Seek Outside Help If Needed:** School counselors, therapists, or supportive relatives can fill gaps when immediate family dynamics are tough.
- **Practice Appreciation:** When a relative listens or respects your boundary, acknowledge it. Positive feedback can encourage them to keep it up.

Good communication does not mean you will never have conflicts. It means you have a better chance of resolving them in a calm, supportive way. Building such habits now can benefit your family relationships not only through your teen years, but well into adulthood.

Chapter 13: Dealing with Grief and Sadness

Loss is something that almost everyone goes through at some point. You might lose a friend due to moving away, experience the passing of a loved one, or watch your parents separate. Grief is the process of reacting to that loss. Sadness, on the other hand, is a feeling that can come and go for many reasons. Sometimes you might feel a deep, heavy sadness that lingers. Other times, you might just have a brief, passing gloomy day. Both grief and sadness can affect how you think and behave, so it is important to know how to recognize them and find ways to cope.

---

1. What Is Grief?

Grief is a natural response to losing someone or something important to you. It can involve a wide range of emotions: sorrow, anger, confusion, or even numbness. Although grief is often associated with death, it can also occur after other types of major losses—like losing a pet, having parents divorce, or ending a close friendship. The depth of your grief usually relates to how important that person or situation was in your life.

Many people describe grief as a process because it can change over time. Early on, you might feel shocked, unable to accept the loss. Later, you could experience waves of sadness or anger. Over time, most people find ways to adjust, even though they may still miss what they lost. Everyone handles grief differently and at their own pace.

---

2. The Difference Between Grief and Sadness

Sadness is a feeling that can arise for many reasons—doing poorly on a test, having an argument with a friend, or simply feeling lonely. It can last for a short time or linger, but sadness does not always link to a major loss. Grief, on the other hand, is usually deeper and more complex. It involves not just sadness, but also a sense that your life has changed or something important has been taken away.

It can be confusing because grief includes sadness as one part of it. However, grief can also involve guilt ("Could I have done something differently?"), anger ("Why did this happen?"), or emptiness ("I feel like part of me is missing."). If you are grieving, it might help to remind yourself that these added emotions are part of the process.

---

3. Common Reactions to Losing Someone or Something

When dealing with a major loss, you may experience reactions in your mind, body, and behavior:

1. **Emotional Reactions:** Feeling numb, hopeless, or even relieved if the situation was complicated. You may cry unexpectedly or feel anger at whoever or whatever caused the loss.
2. **Physical Reactions:** Trouble sleeping, changes in appetite, headaches, or a constant feeling of fatigue can all be physical signs of grief. Your body might respond strongly when it is under emotional stress.
3. **Cognitive Reactions:** Difficulty concentrating, forgetting things, or constantly thinking about the loss can happen. You might replay memories or imagine different outcomes.
4. **Social Reactions:** You may want to isolate yourself, skip events, or not talk to friends. On the other hand, some people prefer to be around others more often for distraction and comfort.

These reactions can come and go in waves. One day you might feel almost normal, and the next day you might be overwhelmed by sorrow again. That is a normal aspect of grieving.

---

4. Misconceptions About Grief

Some people think that grief should follow a neat set of stages, such as denial, anger, sadness, and acceptance, in that exact order. In reality, there is no perfect path. You might feel intense anger one day, then emptiness the next, then go back to anger. Some days, you might not feel much at all, which can be confusing.

Another misconception is that you should "get over it" after a certain amount of time. The truth is, healing from loss does not have a strict deadline. You do not suddenly "stop" grieving on a certain day. Over time, the intense pain often becomes easier to handle, but you might still miss what you lost for years. That does not mean you are failing to move on; it just means the loss mattered deeply to you.

5. How Grief Can Overlap with Depression

Sometimes, it can be difficult to tell the difference between normal grief and clinical depression, because both can involve deep sadness and changes in appetite or sleep. However, depression often includes a strong sense of worthlessness or hopelessness that does not let up, even when good things happen. It can also involve losing interest in activities you used to enjoy, beyond what might be expected from typical grief.

If your sadness and loss of interest continue for many weeks or months, and you cannot function in daily life, consider the possibility that grief has turned into something more. In such cases, reaching out for professional help is an important step. Talking with a counselor or therapist can help you figure out whether you are dealing with extended grief, clinical depression, or both.

6. Ways to Cope with the Loss of a Loved One

When a person close to you dies, your world can feel turned upside down. Here are some approaches that might help:

1. **Allow Yourself to Grieve:** Do not try to push the feelings away or tell yourself you should be "strong" all the time. Crying or feeling down are natural parts of loss.
2. **Seek Support:** Talk with someone you trust—a relative, friend, teacher, or counselor. Sharing memories and emotions can reduce the sense of isolation.
3. **Remember Them in Positive Ways:** You could write a letter to the person, create a small memorial at home, or gather photos that bring good memories.

4. **Continue Routines:** While everything feels different, sticking to some usual routines—like mealtimes or after-school activities—can bring a sense of stability to your day.
5. **Stay Connected with Others:** Even if you do not feel like being around people, try not to shut yourself away completely. Sharing time with understanding friends can remind you that life still has caring connections.
6. **Speak with a Grief Counselor or Join a Group:** Some communities have grief support groups for teens. Meeting peers who have faced similar losses can make you feel less alone.

---

7. Handling Other Types of Loss

Loss is not just about death. You might grieve after a big life change, like moving to a new city, switching schools, or your parents getting divorced. The following suggestions could help:

- **Moving Away:** You might mourn old friends, your room, or familiar places. Try to keep in touch with friends through calls or messages, and allow yourself time to explore your new surroundings.
- **Parents' Separation:** It can feel like the family you knew is gone. Talk to a relative, counselor, or sibling about how you feel. Releasing frustration or sadness in a safe space can help you cope.
- **Friendship Breakup:** When a close friend drifts away or a bond ends, the pain can be intense. Find ways to appreciate the good memories while acknowledging that some relationships do not last forever.

Even though these situations may not involve death, your sadness is real. Give yourself permission to treat it seriously.

---

8. Expressing Sadness Safely

Sadness can be powerful, but there are safe ways to let it out:

1. **Writing:** Keeping a journal or writing letters (even if you do not send them) can help you process feelings.

2. **Art and Music:** Some teens paint, draw, or play instruments to express pain they cannot put into words.
3. **Talking to Someone:** A brief chat with a friend or a longer conversation with a counselor can relieve the weight of sadness.
4. **Physical Outlets:** Activities like running, dancing, or kicking a soccer ball can give emotional energy a place to go.
5. **Allowing Tears:** Crying is a natural release for sadness. It can help you feel calmer afterward.

You might feel pressure to appear okay in front of others, but bottling up sadness often makes it heavier. Finding a healthy outlet can reduce the emotional load.

9. Supporting a Friend Who Is Grieving

You might notice a friend going through loss. Often, people do not know what to say, so they say nothing. But your friend might appreciate simple support:

- **Acknowledge Their Pain:** Saying "I'm here for you" or "I'm sorry for what you're going through" can help them feel seen.
- **Listen More, Talk Less:** Let them guide the conversation. If they want to share memories or cry, be patient and listen.
- **Invite Them to Activities:** Even if they refuse, they may be grateful you asked. Grieving people often need gentle invitations, not isolation.
- **Offer Specific Help:** Instead of "Let me know if you need anything," suggest something concrete like, "Would you like me to come over and watch a movie?"
- **Respect Their Pace:** Grief can last a while. Check in periodically instead of assuming they are fine after a few weeks.

Being present in small ways can be more comforting than trying to "fix" their pain.

10. Dealing with Unresolved Feelings or Regrets

One reason grief can be hard is the feeling that something was left undone or unsaid. You might regret not showing enough appreciation to someone who passed away or feel guilty about an argument you had before they died. These unresolved feelings can weigh heavily on your mind.

- **Write a Letter:** Express everything you wish you could have said. You do not need to send it anywhere; the act of writing can help release guilt or longing.
- **Seek Forgiveness or Closure:** If you feel you need forgiveness (or to forgive them), you can speak to a counselor or trusted adult about how to work through those feelings.
- **Create a Ritual:** Some people find it helpful to light a candle or put a note on a memorial. This symbolic act can help you find personal closure.
- **Remember the Good Times:** Remind yourself of the positive moments in the relationship. Focus on what you did share, rather than what you did not get to do or say.

With time, regrets often fade as you realize no relationship is perfect, and you did what you could under the circumstances.

---

11. Turning Sadness into Reflection

Sometimes, sadness can guide you to reflect on what matters. For instance, if you lose a friend because you took them for granted, your sadness might inspire you to treat the friends you still have with more care. If you are sad because you moved away from a place you loved, you might learn how important a sense of community is to you. This does not mean you have to be "grateful" for sadness, but you can recognize that sorrow can teach you about your values and priorities.

Reflection means paying attention to how sadness affects you and what changes you might want to make. Maybe you decide to spend more time with loved ones or approach relationships with more honesty. While sadness itself is unpleasant, the self-awareness it brings can encourage you to find healthier ways to connect or live.

12. Signs That Professional Help Might Be Needed

Grief and sadness often lessen over time, but there are situations where you might need extra support:

- **Prolonged or Intense Sadness:** If months have passed and you still cannot function in daily tasks, you might be dealing with complicated grief or depression.
- **Self-Harm Thoughts:** If sadness leads you to consider hurting yourself, speak to a trusted adult immediately. These thoughts suggest you need professional care.
- **Substance Abuse:** If you find yourself relying on alcohol or drugs to numb the pain, that is a sign you need help to address the underlying sadness.
- **Severe Changes in Behavior:** Sudden extreme anger, anxiety attacks, or complete social withdrawal can mean you are struggling to cope alone.

A mental health professional—counselor, therapist, or psychiatrist—can help you navigate grief or intense sadness, especially if it is complicated by other factors in your life.

---

13. The Role of Rituals and Remembrance

Many cultures have rituals to help people process grief—like funerals, memorial services, or days to honor deceased relatives. Even if your family does not follow strong traditions, creating your own form of remembrance can be healing. For example:

- **Memory Box:** Keep items that remind you of the person or time you lost. It can be photos, letters, or small belongings.
- **Anniversary Acknowledgments:** On certain days—like the birthday of a loved one who passed away—you might choose to do something symbolic, like lighting a candle or visiting a place they liked.
- **Online Tributes:** Some people set up pages to share memories and photos. This can be comforting if your loved ones or friends live far away.

These rituals do not remove the pain, but they provide a structured way to honor what was lost and acknowledge that the person or place mattered.

14. Handling Sudden Loss

Sometimes, loss strikes without warning—a car accident, a rapid illness, or an unexpected crisis. This kind of sudden loss can bring extra shock and confusion. You might struggle with questions like, "Why them?" or "What if I had done something differently?"

- **Give Yourself Space to Feel Shock:** It is normal to feel numb or disbelieving in the early days. Let yourself process it at your own pace.
- **Lean on Support Quickly:** Sudden loss can be traumatic. Talking to others, even if you are not sure what to say, can help ground you.
- **Seek Crisis Counseling:** If the loss is tied to a violent or traumatic event, specialized counseling might be necessary to work through any resulting fears or nightmares.
- **Avoid Blaming Yourself:** It is common to think, "If only I had been there," but most tragedies are beyond anyone's control. A counselor can help you see that you are not at fault.

15. Continuing Bonds: Staying Connected While Moving Forward

When people say "move on," it can sound like you have to forget the person or situation you lost. However, many grief experts talk about "continuing bonds," which means finding ways to keep a sense of connection without being stuck in the past. For example:

- **Talking to the Lost Person in Your Thoughts:** Some people silently "tell" their loved one about their day or how they are doing.
- **Carrying Their Legacy Forward:** You might do something they cared about, like volunteering at an animal shelter if that was important to them.
- **Keeping a Memento:** A piece of jewelry, a photo in your wallet, or another keepsake can help you feel their presence without preventing you from living your life.

This approach recognizes that the person or the past is still part of who you are, but you can also grow around it.

16. Managing Sadness from Ongoing Situations

Not every loss is clean-cut. Sometimes, you might feel sadness over something that is still happening. For instance, if a family member has a long-term illness, you could be grieving the loss of what life used to be. Or if your parents argue constantly, you might miss the peace you used to know. In these cases:

- **Acknowledge Ambiguous Loss:** Realize that you are grieving the change, not just a final event. This kind of sadness can be ongoing and might need ongoing support.
- **Seek Reliable Allies:** A counselor, friend, or teacher can be a stable place to share your frustrations or fears.
- **Balance Hope and Reality:** It is okay to hope things improve, but also be honest about how you feel right now.
- **Find Comfort in Small Moments:** Even if the overall situation is tough, look for small daily positives—a kind word, a calming hobby, or a relaxing spot to sit.

Coping with ongoing sadness can be draining, so give yourself breaks. Try to engage in activities that uplift you, even if it is only for a short time.

---

17. How Different Ages Grieve

If you have younger siblings or cousins who have also faced a loss, you might notice they handle it differently. Children might express grief through play, or they might ask a lot of questions about death. Older teens might act out or withdraw. There is no single "right" way to show sadness. If you live in a home where multiple people are grieving differently, it can help to be patient with each other. Some might want to talk a lot, while others prefer quiet. Respecting each person's style of grieving can reduce conflicts during an already difficult time.

---

18. Cultural Perspectives on Grief

Different cultures and faiths have unique ways of handling grief. Some hold large ceremonies or gatherings, while others expect mourning to happen quietly. If your culture follows specific practices—like wearing certain colors or holding certain events—participating can give you a sense of structure. On the other hand, if you do not connect strongly to these traditions, you might seek more personal ways of grieving. Either choice can be valid. The key is finding what brings you and your family genuine comfort and respect for the loss.

---

19. Talking to Adults About Your Sadness

If you are dealing with sadness or grief, talking to a trusted adult can help, whether it is a parent, a teacher, a counselor, or a mentor. However, you might fear they will not understand, or you might worry about adding to their stress. Here are some ways to approach it:

- **Choose a Calm Moment:** If possible, pick a time when they are not rushed.
- **Be Direct About Your Feelings:** You could say, "I've been feeling really low since the funeral," or "I'm having trouble coping with the move."
- **Ask for Specific Help:** Maybe you want someone to listen, help you find a counselor, or ease certain responsibilities at home so you have time to grieve.
- **Use Examples:** If you are having trouble sleeping or concentrating, mention that. Concrete details help adults see the seriousness of your feelings.

Even if they cannot solve everything, having an adult who listens can reassure you that you are not alone.

Chapter 14: Recognizing Self-Harm Risks

Feeling sad or hopeless can sometimes lead some people to think about hurting themselves. Self-harm is any act where a person intentionally causes harm to their own body, such as cutting, burning, or hitting themselves. It can also include risky behaviors aimed at punishing oneself. Self-harm is often a way to cope with overwhelming emotions, not necessarily a clear wish to die. However, it is a serious sign that someone is in emotional distress and needs help.

This chapter will explore why teens might turn to self-harm, how to recognize warning signs, and the best steps to take if you or someone you know is thinking of hurting themselves. It is not always easy to talk about self-harm, but understanding it can be a crucial step toward preventing harm and finding healthy ways to deal with pain.

---

1. What Is Self-Harm?

Self-harm involves inflicting physical pain or injury on yourself on purpose. It can take many forms:

- **Cutting:** Using a sharp object to make cuts on the skin, often on the arms or legs.
- **Burning:** Applying something hot to the skin to create burns or marks.
- **Hitting or Banging:** Striking a part of the body against walls or other surfaces.
- **Interfering with Wound Healing:** Picking at scabs or cuts so they do not heal properly.
- **Hair Pulling:** Repeatedly pulling out hair from the scalp or other parts of the body.

Some teens might do this once or twice when overwhelmed, while others might fall into a pattern of repeated self-harm. The reasons can be complex, but it is often linked to feelings of worthlessness, guilt, or a need to release emotional pressure.

2. Why Do Teens Consider Self-Harm?

Teens who self-harm typically struggle with intense emotions or feel they have no other way to handle negative thoughts. Common reasons include:

1. **Temporary Relief:** Some say the physical pain distracts them from overwhelming mental distress.
2. **Punishment:** They might feel they "deserve" pain because of guilt or shame.
3. **Sense of Control:** If life feels chaotic, controlling pain on their own body can seem like taking charge of something.
4. **Communication:** In some cases, self-harm is a way to show others they are in pain because words feel inadequate or scary.
5. **Numbness:** Feeling numb can be distressing, so causing physical harm might make them "feel something" again, even if it is pain.

While self-harm can offer short-term relief or a sense of release, it does not solve the deeper issues. It can also lead to infections, scarring, or accidental severe injury.

---

3. Signs That Someone Might Be Self-Harming

Not everyone who self-harms leaves visible marks, and some might hide injuries under long sleeves or layers of clothes. Still, there are possible clues:

- **Unexplained Injuries:** Cuts, bruises, or burns that the person cannot explain or that seem suspicious.
- **Wearing Covering Clothes in Hot Weather:** They might insist on wearing long sleeves or pants even when it is very warm.
- **Bloodstains on Clothes or Tissues:** You might notice these in the trash, or they might hide them.
- **Possession of Sharp Objects:** Scissors, blades, or other items might be kept in places they did not use before.
- **Frequent Excuses for Injuries:** They might say "Oh, the cat scratched me" or "I tripped" over and over, and the stories might not match the wounds.
- **Withdrawn Behavior and Mood Swings:** If the person is increasingly distant, anxious, or depressed, it can be a sign of deeper distress.

If you spot these signs, it does not always confirm self-harm, but it suggests you should be vigilant and try to provide a safe space for them to talk.

4. Distinguishing Self-Harm from Suicidal Intent

Self-harm is not always an attempt to end one's life. In many cases, it is a coping strategy. However, people who self-harm may also consider suicide, and repeated self-harm can increase the risk of suicidal feelings over time. If a person is talking about wanting to die or is acting recklessly without caring about their safety, it is a signal to seek immediate help.

Understanding the difference can guide how you respond:

- **Self-Harm for Coping:** The teen might injure themselves regularly but does not express a direct desire to die. They might hide the wounds and show relief (not total happiness, but some relief) after self-harm.
- **Suicidal Thoughts or Attempts:** They might say statements like, "I wish I were dead," or "There's no point in living." They may not take steps to treat their injuries after self-harming, or they may talk about wanting their life to end.

In both cases, professional help is crucial. You do not have to figure out alone which category someone falls into. Encourage them to speak with a mental health professional to be safe.

5. How to Talk to Someone Who Self-Harms

If you suspect a friend is hurting themselves, you may feel worried or unsure how to approach them. Here are some tips:

1. **Choose a Private, Calm Setting:** Bring it up when you can have an uninterrupted conversation.
2. **Speak with Compassion:** You could say, "I've noticed some injuries and I'm worried about you. Do you want to talk about what's going on?"

3. **Listen Without Judgment:** Let them express their feelings. Avoid reacting with shock or anger. Show empathy, like, "That sounds really hard. I'm sorry you're feeling this way."
4. **Encourage Professional Help:** Suggest going to a counselor, doctor, or hotline. Offer to help them find resources or accompany them if they feel nervous.
5. **Avoid Ultimatums:** Threatening them—like saying, "If you don't stop, I won't be your friend"—usually drives them deeper into secrecy.
6. **Share Concern with an Adult:** If you think they are in real danger, let a trusted adult know. Keeping it secret might put your friend at greater risk.

Your supportive presence can make a huge difference, but remember that you are not solely responsible for their well-being. They need professional support, too.

---

6. What If You Feel the Urge to Self-Harm?

If you find yourself wanting to hurt your own body, it likely means your emotional pain feels overwhelming. You might not know how else to deal with sadness, anger, or frustration. Here are steps to consider:

- **Pause and Recognize the Urge:** Notice how the thought arises. Are you feeling extreme sadness or stress? Identifying the triggers can help you respond in healthier ways.
- **Use a Delaying Tactic:** Tell yourself you will wait at least five or ten minutes before acting on the urge. In that time, try a coping strategy like calling a friend or doing something calming. Often, the urge can pass or at least lessen.
- **Find Alternatives:** Some people hold ice cubes or snap a rubber band on their wrist to feel a physical sensation without actually cutting or burning themselves. These are not ideal permanent solutions, but they can be safer substitutes when you are desperate.
- **Remove Sharp Objects:** If you can, store them somewhere hard to access, or ask someone you trust to hold onto them. Having them close at hand can make self-harm more likely.

- **Talk to Someone You Trust:** A friend, counselor, or helpline can provide immediate emotional support. Saying out loud how you feel can deflate some of the tension.
- **Seek Professional Help:** Self-harm urges are a sign that you need help learning healthier coping skills. Therapy, counseling, or sometimes medication can be part of a plan to address the root issues.

Remember that you deserve care, and you do not have to handle these urges alone.

---

7. Healthy Coping Strategies for Intense Emotions

For teens who self-harm or are tempted to, developing new ways to cope can be life-changing. Some healthier outlets include:

1. **Relaxation Techniques:** Deep breathing, guided imagery, or muscle relaxation can soothe overwhelming feelings.
2. **Journaling:** Writing about what triggers your urges can help you identify patterns and find solutions.
3. **Physical Activity:** Exercise releases chemicals in the brain that can improve mood. Even a short walk or dance break might help.
4. **Artistic Expression:** Drawing, painting, or playing an instrument can channel emotional energy into creativity.
5. **Talking It Out:** Having a supportive friend or therapist can reduce the sense of isolation that leads to self-harm.
6. **Planning Pleasant Activities:** Watching a funny show, cooking a new recipe, or listening to upbeat music can offer small but meaningful positive experiences.

Coping is about finding what works for you. It might be trial and error. Keep experimenting until you discover techniques that genuinely help you calm down or feel understood.

---

8. Breaking the Cycle of Shame

Shame often fuels self-harm. A teen might feel bad about themselves, self-harm, then feel ashamed for self-harming, and the cycle continues. Recognizing and challenging shame can be crucial:

- **Identify Self-Critical Thoughts:** Phrases like, "I'm worthless," or "I deserve to be hurt," need to be questioned.
- **Practice Self-Compassion:** Talk to yourself as you would talk to a friend. You might say, "I'm in pain right now, and that does not mean I'm a bad person."
- **Challenge Stigma:** Self-harm is often misunderstood. Learning more about its causes might help you see that it is a response to deep emotional distress, not evidence of being "weak."
- **Seek Supportive Environments:** Friends, family, or groups that encourage open conversation can help you replace shame with understanding.

Shame can make you want to hide, but sharing your struggles with a trusted person can gradually weaken its hold.

---

9. The Link Between Trauma and Self-Harm

Self-harm is sometimes a response to past trauma, such as abuse, bullying, or a life-threatening event. If you experienced trauma, you might feel persistent fear, guilt, or a sense of being "tainted" in some way. Self-harm can emerge as a way to manage those overwhelming feelings.

- **Trauma-Focused Therapy:** A counselor trained in trauma can help you process what happened and reduce the emotional triggers that lead to self-harm.
- **Grounding Techniques:** These exercises keep you in the present moment. For example, naming five things you see, four things you can touch, three things you hear, two things you smell, and one thing you taste. This can stop a flashback spiral.
- **Body Awareness Practices:** Gentle exercises like yoga can help you reconnect with your body in a safer, more positive way.

Healing from trauma is a gradual process, but addressing it can significantly reduce the urge to self-harm.

---

10. Talking to Parents or Guardians

You might be scared to tell your parents about self-harm, worried they will be angry or not understand. Still, having an adult on your side can open doors to professional help. Here are tips for starting that conversation:

- **Pick a Calm Moment:** Avoid times when they are busy or stressed. A quiet evening might be best.
- **Explain Your Feelings First:** "I've been feeling really overwhelmed and sad. Sometimes I hurt myself because I don't know how else to cope."
- **Ask for Help, Not Punishment:** Emphasize that you want to find better ways to handle emotions. Suggest seeing a counselor or asking your family doctor for advice.
- **Accept Mixed Reactions:** They might feel scared, upset, or confused. Try to stay calm and let them process. Suggest a follow-up talk or involve a mental health professional.
- **Seek Alternative Adults:** If parents are not supportive, look to a school counselor, relative, or another trusted adult. You still deserve help.

Although it may feel risky, opening up can relieve some of the burden you are carrying alone.

---

11. Seeking Professional Treatment

Various treatment options can help reduce self-harm urges and address the underlying issues:

1. **Therapy or Counseling:** A therapist can teach you coping skills, help you understand emotional triggers, and guide you toward healthier ways to handle stress. Cognitive behavioral therapy (CBT) and dialectical behavior therapy (DBT) are often used to address self-harm.
2. **Medication:** If depression, anxiety, or another mental health condition contributes to self-harm, medication might help stabilize moods and reduce urges. Only a qualified doctor or psychiatrist can decide if medication is right for you.
3. **Support Groups:** Meeting others who have gone through similar struggles can reduce isolation. Many communities and online platforms have groups where members share coping tips and encouragement.

4. **Residential Treatment:** In severe cases, a short stay at a mental health facility might be needed if there is a high risk of serious harm. This can provide 24-hour support and safety.

Professional treatment is not an instant fix, but it can guide you step by step toward fewer self-harm episodes and healthier emotional expression.

---

12. Supporting a Friend Who Admits Self-Harm

If a friend confides in you about their self-harm, it is common to feel panicked or unsure. Here is how you can help:

- **Stay Calm and Listen:** Let them share their feelings without interruption.
- **Encourage Professional Help:** You might say, "I care about you, and I think it would help to talk to a counselor. Can I go with you to the school counselor's office?"
- **Offer to Remove Harmful Items:** If they feel unsafe at a certain moment, helping them clear out sharp objects can reduce the immediate risk.
- **Know Your Limits:** You can be supportive, but you are not their therapist. Gently suggest involving an adult or mental health professional.
- **Check In Regularly:** A simple text or call can remind them they are not alone. But do not put all the responsibility on yourself.

Being there for someone who self-harms can be emotionally taxing. Make sure you also have someone to talk to about your own worries and feelings.

---

13. Myths About Self-Harm

Several myths can make it harder to understand self-harm:

- **"They're Just Seeking Attention."** Some people say self-harm is a way to get attention. In reality, most teens hide their injuries and do not want others to know. If someone shows or mentions their self-harm, it might be a cry for help, which still deserves compassion and support.
- **"Only Girls Do It."** Self-harm can affect anyone, regardless of gender. Boys often face extra stigma about expressing emotional pain, so they might hide it more.

- **"It's Just a Phase."** Self-harm can become an addictive pattern. Even if some teens stop on their own, many need professional help to manage the emotional problems behind it.
- **"They Must Want to Die."** While self-harm is serious, it is not always a suicide attempt. However, it does raise the risk that someone could harm themselves more seriously over time.

Learning the facts can help you respond appropriately if you or someone else is dealing with self-harm.

14. Practical Distractions in Crisis Moments

When the urge to self-harm hits, having a list of distractions can be lifesaving:

1. **Call a Helpline:** Hearing a calm voice can ground you.
2. **Hold Something Cold or Warm:** Gripping an ice pack or hugging a warm water bottle can create a physical sensation without injury.
3. **Write Down All the Reasons You Should Stay Safe:** Even if they feel weak in the moment, it can help shift your focus.
4. **Breathing Exercises:** Count in for four seconds, hold for four, and out for four. Repeat until the sharp urge subsides.
5. **Engage in a Task:** Wash dishes, draw a random picture, do a puzzle—anything to buy time and distract yourself.

Prepare this list ahead of time and keep it accessible, like on your phone or in a small notebook.

15. Long-Term Strategies for Preventing Relapse

Overcoming self-harm does not end with stopping the behavior once. You might experience setbacks, especially during stressful times. Ongoing prevention involves:

- **Recognizing Triggers:** Note the situations or thoughts that stir up the urge. Plan what to do when triggers happen again.

- **Staying in Therapy (If Possible):** Regular sessions can support you as you navigate day-to-day problems and keep learning new coping skills.
- **Building a Support Network:** Let close friends, family, or mentors know you have struggled before, so they can keep an eye on you if you show signs of slipping back.
- **Practicing Self-Care:** Keep up healthy eating, sleep routines, and some physical activity. These basic habits support emotional balance.
- **Rewarding Progress:** Recognize each step you take toward healthier coping. Even small steps, like talking about your feelings once instead of self-harming, are important to keep in mind.

Recovery is a process. Slipping up now and then does not mean you have failed. It is a signal that you might need extra support or to revisit certain strategies.

---

16. When Hospital Care Might Be Needed

Sometimes, the risk of severe harm is high. This could be due to:

- **Extreme Suicidal Thoughts:** You have a detailed plan or strong desire to end your life.
- **Severe Injuries:** You harm yourself in ways that need immediate medical attention or show a lack of concern for your safety.
- **Lack of Self-Control:** You feel unable to resist self-harm urges despite using coping strategies or therapy.

In these cases, a short hospital stay or crisis intervention center might be the safest option. While it can feel scary to enter a hospital, the purpose is to stabilize you and protect you while you get further support.

---

17. Cultural or Community Factors

In some communities, mental health struggles carry a stigma. Teens may feel they cannot share self-harm issues because people might judge them or their family. Others might come from backgrounds where strong emotions are kept private. If this applies to you:

- **Look for Specialized Resources:** Some counseling centers understand the challenges of talking about self-harm in certain cultural settings.
- **Seek Online Support (Cautiously):** If local resources are limited, online helplines or therapy can offer a starting point.
- **Confide in a Mentor:** A coach, spiritual leader, or teacher might be more understanding than you expect.
- **Challenge Stigma Gently:** If someone dismisses self-harm as "attention-seeking," you can share basic facts. Remember, you have the right to seek help regardless of social judgments.

---

18. The Role of Schools in Prevention

Many schools are now more aware of mental health issues. Guidance counselors, school psychologists, or social workers can be valuable resources. If you are a student feeling the urge to self-harm, consider:

- **Visiting the School Counselor:** They can offer a private space to talk and point you to local resources.
- **Talking to a Teacher You Trust:** They might help you reach the right professional in the school system.
- **Peer Support Programs:** Some schools have peer mentoring groups that give students a safe place to share and learn coping skills.

These school-based supports are there for a reason—do not be afraid to use them, even if it feels uncomfortable at first.

---

19. Recovery and Hope

Self-harm can trap you in a cycle of shame and despair, but many teens do recover. They find new ways to handle emotions, build self-esteem, and heal relationships. Over time, the urge to self-harm can weaken. It might still show up in moments of extreme stress, but with practice, you can learn to ride through those moments without harming yourself.

Recovery often involves:

- **Therapeutic Techniques:** Tools like DBT's "emotion regulation" skills help you understand and manage strong feelings.
- **Supportive Relationships:** Friends, family, or mentors who respect your struggle and encourage you to keep trying.
- **Personal Growth:** Learning about your triggers, building confidence, and finding meaningful goals that give you a sense of purpose.

Even if you have tried to stop before and relapsed, you can still move forward. Each attempt at healthier coping teaches you more about what works for you.

20. Moving Toward a Safer Future

Self-harm is a serious issue, but it does not define you. Recognizing the risks and learning to spot the warning signs—whether in yourself or others—can prevent deeper harm. By speaking up, seeking help, and exploring alternative ways to handle emotional pain, you open a path to a safer, healthier life.

If you worry you might harm yourself or see signs in a friend, do not hesitate to reach out to an adult, counselor, or mental health professional. It can be frightening to admit self-harm, but getting help is a courageous choice. With appropriate support, it is possible to replace self-destructive impulses with coping skills that respect and protect your well-being.

Conclusion

Self-harm often arises from an intense desire to ease or express overwhelming emotional pain. While it might provide momentary relief, it leads to more problems in the long run, including physical harm and the possibility of deeper emotional distress. Recognizing the signs—such as hidden injuries, mood swings, or possession of sharp objects—can help you intervene early if a friend is in danger. If you are the one struggling, know that it is not your fault and that you are not alone. Professionals, hotlines, counselors, and trustworthy adults can help guide you toward better coping methods. Change is possible. By taking the step to talk about self-harm, you are moving closer to safety and emotional healing.

Chapter 15: Habits That May Worsen Depression

Depression is a serious condition that can affect how you think, feel, and behave. It can make everyday life feel challenging. While there are various causes of depression—ranging from brain chemistry to stressful life events—certain habits can keep you stuck in a low mood or even make it worse. You might not realize that some things you do every day are adding extra weight to your sadness or hopelessness. By identifying unhelpful habits and learning how they affect you, you can start to replace them with healthier patterns. This chapter explores common habits that may worsen depression and offers suggestions for more supportive ways to manage your well-being.

1. Avoiding or Ignoring Emotions

Many people feel uncomfortable with deep or painful emotions. They might try to push them away or pretend they do not exist. While it might seem easier to ignore sadness, anger, or guilt, burying these feelings can keep them from being processed. Over time, they can pile up and contribute to ongoing low mood.

- **Why It Worsens Depression:** When you avoid emotions, you lose the chance to address their causes. Unresolved feelings can continue to simmer under the surface, feeding negative thought patterns.
- **What to Do Instead:** Give yourself permission to acknowledge emotions without judging them. You might journal briefly or talk with someone you trust. Naming a feeling can make it more manageable, even if it does not go away right away. Recognizing that it is normal to have tough emotions can reduce shame or guilt about feeling low.

2. Engaging in Negative Self-Talk

Your thoughts can strongly influence your feelings and actions. If you regularly call yourself names ("I'm stupid," "I'm worthless") or assume everything is your fault, you create an environment inside your mind where depressive ideas thrive. Over time, this negative self-talk can feel normal, making it harder to see any positive qualities in yourself or the world.

- **Why It Worsens Depression:** Negative self-talk can convince you that you cannot change or that you have no value. This hopeless outlook is a known factor in deepening depression.
- **What to Do Instead:** Practice spotting negative thoughts as they appear. Ask yourself if they are fully true or if there might be a more balanced way to see the situation. For instance, if you think, "I mess everything up," try to recall times when you did a task well. Even small successes can challenge blanket statements about your failure. It takes time to shift negative self-talk, but repeating more accurate or compassionate thoughts can slowly weaken the grip of harsh inner voices.

---

3. Isolating Yourself from Others

When you feel down, you might lose the energy or desire to be around people. Maybe you worry they will not understand your sadness, or you feel too tired to keep up a conversation. Isolation can become a habit, and the more you avoid social contact, the more comfortable you become with being alone. However, too much time in solitude can feed into a cycle of loneliness and deeper depression.

- **Why It Worsens Depression:** Humans are social creatures, and supportive relationships often act as a buffer against low mood. Without connections, you may have no one to confide in when things feel heavy. Loneliness can then amplify negative thoughts.
- **What to Do Instead:** You do not have to attend big parties or force yourself into situations that feel overwhelming. A smaller step could be texting one friend or joining an online group focused on an interest you care about. Short, comfortable interactions can help maintain some social ties. Over time, you might find it easier to gradually increase the amount of contact you have with others.

---

4. Disrupted or Inadequate Sleep

Sleep plays a big role in mental health. Depression can cause changes in sleep—some people sleep much more than before, while others cannot fall asleep or stay asleep. But even when depression leads you to want more rest, that sleep is not always restorative if your schedule is out of sync. If you stay up very late browsing on your phone or do not maintain a consistent sleep routine, you may feel groggy and irritated the next day, which can worsen depression.

- **Why It Worsens Depression:** Lack of quality sleep can heighten stress, make it harder to regulate emotions, and reduce your ability to handle daily tasks. Also, poor sleep often interferes with concentration and memory, which can add frustration to an already low mood.
- **What to Do Instead:** Aim for a steady bedtime and wake-up time if possible. Avoid bright screens or intense activities right before bedtime. If you have trouble sleeping, you might try calming routines like taking a warm shower, reading, or doing gentle stretches. Small steps such as these can help your body recognize when it is time to wind down.

---

5. Relying on Unhealthy Coping Mechanisms

When sadness or stress becomes overwhelming, people sometimes turn to habits that numb the pain for a short while but do more harm in the long run. Substance abuse (like alcohol or illegal drugs), self-harm, or even overuse of social media can give brief escapes. However, these habits typically do not address the root issues and can make you feel worse afterward.

- **Why It Worsens Depression:** Substances, for instance, can alter your brain chemistry, leading to temporary relief followed by a crash that intensifies low feelings. Self-harm poses serious physical and emotional risks. Overusing social media can lead to comparison with others, fueling negative self-perceptions.
- **What to Do Instead:** Seek healthier outlets for emotional pain. This might include talking with a trusted individual, engaging in hobbies, or trying relaxation techniques. It is not easy to break from unhealthy coping strategies, especially if they have become routines. Professional help may be needed to learn more effective methods.

---

6. Overconsumption of Media and Technology

Scrolling through social media feeds, watching videos late into the night, or constantly checking news updates can turn into a habit that occupies hours of your day. While it can be a distraction, this constant online activity might end up fueling negative feelings or anxieties, especially if you see content that triggers sadness or envy.

- **Why It Worsens Depression:** Comparison with others—seeing perfect selfies, vacations, or achievements—can deepen the sense of "I'm not doing well enough." Negative news or online arguments can heighten hopelessness or irritability.
- **What to Do Instead:** Set boundaries for media use. Perhaps schedule certain times for checking social feeds or reading news. Turn off notifications so you are not pulled in every few minutes. Consider replacing some screen time with an offline activity—reading a physical book, drawing, or playing a musical instrument. This balance can reduce the mental load caused by non-stop content consumption.

---

7. Consuming Too Much Junk Food

Your diet can affect how you feel both physically and emotionally. Eating a lot of sugary snacks, fast food, or heavily processed meals might give a quick energy burst but often leads to a crash. Lack of nutrients can also influence mood and energy levels, making it harder to handle stress or sadness in a balanced way.

- **Why It Worsens Depression:** Quick sugar highs end in crashes that can leave you feeling more fatigued or moody. A poor diet can also contribute to physical health problems, which in turn may lower your overall sense of well-being.
- **What to Do Instead:** You do not have to eliminate all treats, but adding healthier options—like fruits, vegetables, or whole grains—can provide your body with needed vitamins and steady energy. Drinking enough water and eating balanced meals can support brain function and make it a little easier to navigate tough emotional states.

8. Inactivity and Lack of Movement

When feeling depressed, the idea of exercise might seem overwhelming. You might prefer staying in bed or on the couch, finding comfort in stillness. However, complete inactivity can maintain low mood because your body does not get the benefits of movement, such as improved blood flow and the release of mood-boosting chemicals.

- **Why It Worsens Depression:** Physical inactivity can contribute to lower energy, stiffer muscles, and poor cardiovascular health. It can also leave more time for ruminating on negative thoughts.
- **What to Do Instead:** You do not need a heavy workout routine. Start small—maybe a slow walk around the block or a simple stretch session in your room. Gradually, you might find you can do a bit more. Even short, gentle movement can help break up the day, improve circulation, and release helpful neurotransmitters that can slightly lift your mood.

---

9. Procrastinating Important Tasks

Putting off homework, chores, or personal projects is easy to do when you lack motivation, but piling up tasks can create more stress. As deadlines loom, you might feel even more anxious or down on yourself for not getting things done. This cycle of procrastination and guilt can deepen a sense of failure.

- **Why It Worsens Depression:** Missed deadlines or incomplete responsibilities can hurt your self-esteem and feed the idea that you cannot succeed. It also leaves problems unresolved, adding to mental clutter.
- **What to Do Instead:** Break tasks into smaller, more manageable steps. Even a short burst of productivity—like working on a paper for 10 minutes—can help you feel you have made progress. Keep a simple checklist or planner to track what you have accomplished. This visual reminder of completed tasks can push back against the belief that you "never do anything right."

10. Overspending or Impulse Shopping

Some teens turn to shopping (online or in person) as a quick pick-me-up. Getting new items might offer a brief thrill or sense of excitement. However, impulse purchases can lead to financial stress (even if it is just your allowance) and clutter, which can raise stress levels over time.

- **Why It Worsens Depression:** Guilt or regret after buying unnecessary items can feed negative self-talk, especially if you realize you wasted money or never really wanted those items.
- **What to Do Instead:** Pause before buying. Ask yourself if you need the item or if it is just a way to feel better momentarily. Consider waiting 24 hours before making the purchase. During that time, the urge to buy might pass, or you may find a free alternative for the same enjoyment, like borrowing a book from the library or using free online resources.

---

11. Constant Self-Criticism in Front of Others

Sometimes, teens use self-deprecating humor around friends or downplay their own achievements because they do not want to appear conceited. While occasional self-mockery might seem harmless, repeatedly putting yourself down in front of others can reinforce your own low view of yourself. It also teaches others that you see yourself as lesser or unworthy.

- **Why It Worsens Depression:** Speaking negatively about yourself, even as a joke, can become a habit that cements negative beliefs in your own mind. It invites others to view you in that light, too, which could weaken your support system if they do not realize you need genuine encouragement.
- **What to Do Instead:** Pay attention to how you talk about yourself. If you notice a pattern of harsh, self-critical jokes, experiment with a neutral or slightly positive statement. For example, instead of saying, "I'm a total loser at sports," you might say, "Sports aren't my strong point, but I like watching games." This might feel strange at first, but it can help shift your internal self-image over time.

12. Skipping Appointments or Medication

If you have been prescribed medication for depression or have scheduled therapy sessions, missing them can disrupt your progress. Some people skip appointments because they are not in the mood, do not feel they are improving quickly enough, or worry they will be judged. Stopping medication on your own can also lead to withdrawal symptoms or a return of severe symptoms.

- **Why It Worsens Depression:** Therapies and medications often require consistent use to be effective. Interruptions in treatment can delay improvement or even worsen your condition.
- **What to Do Instead:** Communicate openly with your doctor or therapist if you feel the treatment is not helping or if side effects bother you. They can adjust dosages, suggest alternate therapies, or explore different approaches. Consistency is key in managing depression, so work with professionals instead of making changes on your own.

---

13. Taking On Too Many Obligations

While some people under-function when depressed, others do the opposite: they fill every minute with tasks or responsibilities in an attempt to escape negative thoughts. This constant busyness can lead to burnout. When the energy runs out, you might crash, feeling even more depressed because you cannot keep up with an overpacked schedule.

- **Why It Worsens Depression:** Exhaustion and stress lower your ability to cope with normal ups and downs. Overcommitment can also rob you of downtime you might need to rest or reflect.
- **What to Do Instead:** Look at your schedule and see if there are any activities you can postpone or drop. It is okay to set boundaries and say "no" sometimes. Balancing responsibilities with relaxation can help you conserve emotional and physical energy for what truly matters.

---

14. Endless Rumination on Negative Events

Rumination means replaying negative experiences or worries in your mind. You might go over a past mistake repeatedly, wondering what you could have done differently. Or you might fixate on a fear about the future, imagining worst-case scenarios. This mental loop can become a habit, making it tough to find relief from negative thoughts.

- **Why It Worsens Depression:** Rumination keeps the emotional wounds open, preventing you from moving on or focusing on present tasks. It can fuel self-blame or hopelessness.
- **What to Do Instead:** Try "thought-stopping" techniques. When you notice yourself going down the same painful mental track, deliberately shift your attention to another activity, like a puzzle or a simple physical exercise. Over time, you can train your mind to recognize rumination and interrupt it before it deepens your despair.

---

15. Criticizing Yourself for Feeling Depressed

You might believe that feeling depressed means you are weak or failing at life. Criticizing yourself for having these feelings can add another layer of shame or anger. It can also discourage you from seeking help, because you think you should "just get over it" on your own.

- **Why It Worsens Depression:** This mindset blocks compassion for yourself at a time when you most need understanding. It may also lead you to hide your depression, missing out on support from friends, family, or professionals.
- **What to Do Instead:** Remind yourself that depression is not a choice or a character flaw. If you had a broken arm, you would not blame yourself for the injury; you would seek proper care. Treat mental health the same way. Recognize that reaching out or talking about your feelings is a brave step, not a sign of weakness.

---

16. Inability to Accept Help

When someone offers support—a friend suggesting a walk, a parent offering to listen, or a counselor providing advice—you might refuse because you believe nobody can help or that you do not deserve help. Pushing away assistance can leave you isolated, with no relief from the weight you carry.

- **Why It Worsens Depression:** Isolation and hopelessness grow when you resist help. You might miss opportunities for connection or guidance that could ease some of your burdens.
- **What to Do Instead:** Practice openness. Even if a suggestion (like going for a brief walk) seems small, give it a chance. If it truly does not help, you can let the other person know, but at least you remain open to trying. Accepting help does not make you a burden; it is a sign that you recognize your own worth and right to feel better.

---

17. Allowing Guilt to Take Over

Depression sometimes involves guilt: guilt for not being productive, guilt for feeling sad, guilt for disappointing others. In small doses, guilt can push you to make amends. But persistent guilt that you cannot resolve can weigh you down, reinforcing a belief that you are always at fault.

- **Why It Worsens Depression:** Excessive guilt can merge with negative self-talk, forming a view of yourself as bad or unforgivable. This deepens hopelessness and can keep you from addressing what is truly bothering you.
- **What to Do Instead:** If there is something concrete you can do to fix a situation—like apologizing or making up for a missed duty—take that step. If the guilt is more general, talk it through with someone who can offer a reality check. They might help you see that you are being too hard on yourself. Learning to forgive yourself for being human is an important piece of managing depression.

---

18. Constantly Trying to Face Everything Alone

It can be tempting to believe that you must handle all emotional battles on your own. Maybe you do not want to trouble anyone, or you think you should be able to cope by sheer willpower. Depression, however, can become heavier when you isolate yourself from available support.

- **Why It Worsens Depression:** Facing big emotional challenges without outside perspective or assistance can trap you in your own negative

patterns. You might miss solutions or coping strategies that others can suggest.
- **What to Do Instead:** Even if it feels uncomfortable, reach out to at least one person. It could be a friend, family member, teacher, or counselor. Sharing your thoughts can provide relief and open doors to resources you did not know about. Sometimes, just knowing someone is rooting for you can improve your outlook.

---

19. Resisting Any Sort of Change

Depression can make you feel exhausted. Trying new strategies—like going to therapy, altering your sleep routine, or starting a mild exercise plan—can seem like an impossible task. You might think, "What's the point?" However, staying locked in the same routines that contribute to your low mood usually prolongs or worsens depression.

- **Why It Worsens Depression:** If current patterns are fueling your sadness, keeping them the same means nothing improves. Over time, the feeling of stagnation can confirm the hopeless idea that you are stuck forever.
- **What to Do Instead:** Start with very small adjustments. Maybe that is going to bed 15 minutes earlier or taking a short walk once a week. Even minor changes can introduce a fresh sense of possibility. If you see a little improvement, you might be more motivated to try another new step. Over time, these incremental changes can accumulate to create noticeable differences in your overall mood.

---

20. Overlooking the Value of Professional Care

Depression is not always something you can simply wish away. Left unchecked, it can become deeply entrenched. Some people resist seeing a counselor, therapist, or doctor because they worry about stigma or fear that their concerns are not "serious enough." Others might have had a bad experience with one therapist and decide no help is possible.

- **Why It Worsens Depression:** Without qualified support, you may not learn effective coping methods or receive the medical assistance (such as

medication) that could stabilize your mood. This can lead to ongoing problems in school, relationships, or physical health.
- **What to Do Instead:** Acknowledge that professional help is a form of self-care. Even if you have doubts, give it a try. Not every therapist or doctor is the right fit, so do not be discouraged if the first one does not match your personality or needs. Keep searching until you find someone you trust. Depression is treatable, and professional guidance often plays a key role in recovery.

Putting It All Together

Habits that worsen depression can develop slowly, sometimes without you even realizing it. Small daily choices—like neglecting sleep, dwelling on negative thoughts, or spending hours scrolling through social media—can pile up, fueling low mood and reinforcing hopelessness. But just as these habits can maintain depression, addressing them can also open the door to improvement.

Here are some steps to keep in mind:

1. **Recognize Harmful Patterns:** Reflect on your day-to-day behavior. Notice if you rely on any of the habits described here.
2. **Start with One Change:** You do not have to overhaul your entire life overnight. Pick one habit, such as your sleep schedule or negative self-talk, and focus on making small adjustments.
3. **Seek Support:** Talk to friends, family members, or professionals about your efforts. They can offer tips, encouragement, or accountability.
4. **Be Patient with Yourself:** Changing habits takes time, especially when you are already struggling with low energy. Celebrate small wins, and understand that minor setbacks do not mean failure.

Depression might create the illusion that nothing will help, but altering harmful habits can gradually lift some of the emotional weight. While making these changes will not always instantly make you feel better, each step can build momentum toward healthier patterns. Combined with professional treatment, social support, and personal awareness, tackling unhelpful habits is an important part of finding steadier emotional ground.

Chapter 16: Setting Reasonable Goals

Goals can give direction in life. They can motivate you to learn new skills, keep you focused on something positive, and boost your sense of achievement. However, when you are depressed, the very idea of setting goals might feel intimidating. You might fear failure, lack the energy to follow through, or worry that no goals matter because you do not see a bright future. Despite these challenges, learning how to choose and work toward reasonable goals can be a valuable strategy for managing depression. This chapter will explore why goal-setting matters, how it can support mental health, and how to set goals in a way that is realistic and uplifting rather than overwhelming.

---

1. Why Goals Can Help

When you are feeling low, a sense of aimlessness can take over. You might wake up not knowing what you are working toward, making each day feel repetitive or pointless. Goals introduce a sense of purpose, however small. They remind you that there are tasks you can achieve, even if you do not feel your best.

- **Focus:** Goals help you direct your limited energy toward something specific, reducing random negative thinking.
- **Hope:** Having something to aim for can challenge the hopelessness that depression brings. Completing a step—no matter how minor—can provide a glimmer of optimism.
- **Structure:** Goals give your day a framework. If you know you want to spend 15 minutes reading a new book, you have a mini-target to plan around.

Of course, goals alone will not cure depression, but they can form part of a supportive environment for healing when combined with other strategies like therapy, social support, and healthy self-care.

---

2. Common Pitfalls in Goal-Setting for Depressed Teens

When depressed, certain mistakes in choosing goals can worsen your mood. Being aware of these pitfalls can help you avoid them:

1. **Setting Goals That Are Too Big:** For example, deciding you will transform your grades from all low marks to perfect scores in just a week. Such a major leap can feel impossible and lead to more discouragement.
2. **Comparing Yourself to Others:** You might pick goals solely because you see friends achieving them. But your situation is unique, and what works for someone else might be too much or too little for you.
3. **Lack of Flexibility:** Believing you must stick to a goal no matter what can create stress if your energy or circumstances shift. Sometimes you need to adjust your aim.
4. **Ignoring Small Wins:** You may focus on what you have not accomplished yet, overlooking the little steps you have already taken.

Recognizing these tendencies allows you to approach goal-setting in a more nurturing way, reducing the risk of feeling overwhelmed.

---

3. Understanding Your Current Limits

Depression often brings fatigue, brain fog, or emotional instability. Demanding that you meet the same standards as someone who is not depressed can set you up for failure. It is important to gauge where you are right now, not where you think you "should" be.

- **Physical Energy:** Notice how tired you feel during the day. If you struggle to get out of bed, setting a goal of exercising daily might be too big a jump.
- **Time Constraints:** If you have school, family duties, or a part-time job, your free hours might be limited. Choose goals that fit the time you realistically have.
- **Emotional Readiness:** Some goals might trigger anxiety or sadness. If you are not ready to tackle a huge fear, start with a smaller, related step.

Being honest about your capacity is not admitting defeat. It is about matching goals to your actual situation, which increases the chance of success.

---

4. Learning About SMART Goals

One common method for creating workable goals is the "SMART" framework. While you do not have to follow it strictly, it can guide you in being more concrete:

- **S (Specific):** Instead of "I'll get better at math," try "I'll complete two math practice problems each day after school."
- **M (Measurable):** Ensure you can tell if you met the goal. For instance, "two math problems" is clear; you either did them or did not.
- **A (Achievable):** Ask if it is within your capability right now. If you are failing math entirely, you might start with reviewing one topic rather than tackling advanced problems.
- **R (Relevant):** The goal should make sense for your life and mood. If improving math skills helps you feel more confident, that is relevant.
- **T (Time-Bound):** Give yourself a timeframe, like "this week" or "by Friday." Without a time limit, goals can drift and feel less motivating.

For depressed teens, you might want to keep each step very small. A micro-goal that seems almost trivial can still provide a sense of progress.

---

5. Picking Goals That Align with Personal Interests

Goals can be about more than just academic tasks or chores. They can also involve hobbies, relationships, or mental health practices. If you choose something you genuinely find interesting, you are more likely to follow through even when your mood is low.

- **Creative Outlets:** If you enjoy drawing, set a goal to sketch for five minutes a day.
- **Physical Activities:** If you like certain sports or dancing, set a small goal related to that, like practicing a certain move or routine twice a week.
- **Personal Growth:** Perhaps you want to learn a new skill, like basic cooking or a few phrases in a foreign language.
- **Social Interaction:** If you feel isolated, you might aim to message one friend every evening or attend one school club meeting a week.

Focusing on things that naturally spark your interest can serve as a buffer against total apathy.

6. Breaking Goals into Smaller Steps

If a goal looks too big, your depressed mind might immediately scream, "Impossible!" Breaking the goal into tiny steps can help. For example, if you want to raise your math grade:

1. **Step 1:** Organize your notebook.
2. **Step 2:** Identify which chapters you do not understand.
3. **Step 3:** Ask a teacher or classmate for tips.
4. **Step 4:** Practice 15 minutes of problems on just one topic.
5. **Step 5:** Reward yourself with a small treat or break.

By focusing on one small piece at a time, you reduce the chance of feeling overwhelmed. Even a five- or ten-minute commitment can be enough to keep you moving forward.

---

7. Setting Timeframes That Encourage Action

Long-term goals like "I want to become a doctor" can be inspirational, but they might be too far away to provide day-to-day motivation, especially when you are depressed. Mixing in short-term goals—like finishing this week's homework or reading one chapter of a certain book—can give a sense of accomplishment sooner.

- **Immediate Goals (Daily/Weekly):** These keep you moving and offer quick wins.
- **Mid-Range Goals (Monthly/Quarterly):** These might involve noticing progress, such as improving a grade by one letter or finishing half of a personal project.
- **Long-Term Hopes (Year or More):** You can keep these in mind as a guiding light, but do not let them overshadow the smaller steps that make everyday life manageable.

Having timeframes that span from a few days to a few months can reduce the all-or-nothing feeling and allow you to see gradual advancement.

8. Allowing Room for Adjustments

Depression can fluctuate. Some days you might feel more energized, while others you can barely get out of bed. If you rigidly stick to a plan that does not account for these ups and downs, you risk feeling like a failure on tougher days. Flexibility can help you avoid harsh self-criticism.

- **Why Adjustments Help:** Life events—like a family conflict or extra stress at school—may require shifting your priorities. If you blame yourself every time a goal needs to change, you add unnecessary guilt.
- **How to Adjust:** Maybe you planned to practice guitar for 30 minutes, but you only managed 10 minutes. Instead of seeing it as a failure, acknowledge that you did something. If needed, shift your 30-minute goal to a different day or break it into smaller 10-minute sessions.

Being adaptable can keep you from giving up altogether.

---

9. Combining Goals with Self-Care Practices

Working toward goals takes mental energy, which can be limited when you are depressed. To prevent burnout, pair goal-setting with self-care. For instance, if you plan to study for 30 minutes, also schedule a short break to stretch or breathe deeply. If you aim to improve your fitness, make sure you also rest and not push yourself to exhaustion.

- **Balanced Approach:** Goals should not drain you completely. Instead, they should coexist with strategies that replenish your emotional reserves.
- **Reward Yourself:** After completing a step, treat yourself to something relaxing or fun—maybe a short phone call with a friend, a favorite snack, or some time with a calming hobby.

This balance helps ensure goals do not become yet another source of stress.

---

10. Tracking Progress in a Visible Way

When you are depressed, it is easy to forget achievements and focus on what is still lacking. Keeping a small record of completed steps can remind you that you are indeed making moves in a positive direction, no matter how small they may seem.

- **Journal or Planner:** You can jot down each day's completed tasks or short goals. Looking back after a week can show that you have done more than you realized.
- **Apps or Habit Trackers:** Many apps let you mark off daily goals—like drinking enough water or practicing a hobby. The visual checkmarks can offer a tiny sense of satisfaction.
- **Bulletin Board or Paper List:** Even just a piece of paper on your wall where you write "Finished today's math problem!" can be uplifting.

This tangible evidence combats the distorted belief that you "never accomplish anything."

---

11. Using Support Systems

You do not have to set or pursue goals alone. Friends, family members, or mentors can help you choose realistic aims, give you feedback, and cheer you on when you make progress. Sometimes just telling someone, "I plan to do X by Friday," can create accountability that motivates you to follow through.

- **Check-In Buddy:** Ask a friend or sibling if they can do a quick check-in about your goals once or twice a week. They do not have to fix your problems, just see how you are doing.
- **Study Groups or Peer Groups:** If your goal is academic, a study group can keep you on track. If your goal is creative, a club or group that shares the hobby can be encouraging.
- **Professional Guidance:** A counselor or therapist can help you set goals that match your mental health needs. They can also help you explore blockages when you feel stuck.

Letting supportive people be part of your goal process can ease the isolation that often comes with depression.

12. Addressing Fear of Failure

One big obstacle is the worry that you will not meet your goals, leading to more disappointment. This fear can be paralyzing. But refusing to try can lock you in a place where nothing improves. Learning to accept the possibility of imperfection can make goal-setting less daunting.

- **Reframing Failure:** Not meeting a goal once does not mean you are incapable. It can be a signal that the goal needs adjusting or that you faced unexpected obstacles.
- **Small Safety Nets:** Instead of one big, high-stakes goal, set smaller sub-goals. If one does not work out, you can succeed at another. This diversifies your sense of achievement.
- **Self-Kindness in Mistakes:** If you fail or fall short, talk to yourself in a gentle way. "It's okay. I tried. Now I can see what went wrong and possibly do better next time."

Overcoming fear of failure is about allowing yourself room to learn rather than punishing yourself for not being perfect.

---

13. Making Goals That Reflect Emotional Needs

Goals do not have to be about grades or material achievements. They can also focus on emotional well-being. For instance, you might set a goal to speak kindly to yourself at least once a day. Or you could aim to practice a relaxation technique every evening before bed.

- **Examples of Emotional Goals:**
    - Write one positive thing about yourself in a journal daily.
    - Try a simple breathing exercise when you wake up and before you go to sleep.
    - Spend 10 minutes doing a calming activity like coloring or listening to relaxing music.

These emotional or mental health–centered goals ensure you are actively working on improving how you feel, not just ticking off tasks that might not address your internal state.

14. Handling Setbacks Without Giving Up

Depression can cause good days and bad days. Sometimes you will be on a roll, completing tasks or making progress. Other times you might slip back into low motivation and do little for a week. This does not erase your previous progress. It is a common pattern in managing depression.

- **Practical Steps for Setbacks:**
    1. **Acknowledge Emotions:** It is okay to feel disappointed or frustrated.
    2. **Assess the Situation:** What factors contributed to the setback? Was it extra stress at home, a poor night's sleep, or maybe an argument with a friend?
    3. **Revise Goals if Needed:** Adjust timelines or reduce the scale of the goal to match your current mood.
    4. **Self-Compassion:** Remind yourself that setbacks happen in all sorts of goals—academic, athletic, or personal. You can keep going.

This approach stops a temporary fall from turning into a permanent stop.

---

15. Tying Goals to Meaningful Values

When depressed, you might ask, "What is the point?" Having a reason behind a goal can help you see its importance. Perhaps you want to do better in school not just for the grade, but because you want to prove to yourself you can learn. Or you might clean your room regularly because you value a calm environment that supports better sleep.

- **Finding Personal Meaning:** Think about what matters to you—kindness, creativity, personal growth, or helping others. Link your goals to these values. For instance, if you value kindness, set a goal to do one kind act a day.
- **Long-Term Perspective:** Even if you do not see immediate benefits, remember your broader motivations. For example, being consistent with studying might open future opportunities, or developing a hobby might bring a sense of personal pride.

Clarity on why a goal matters can counter the low energy or skepticism depression can generate.

16. Small Steps

Many people with depression downplay their successes, thinking, "It's not a big deal" or "Anyone could have done that." Yet acknowledging even small achievements can build momentum. If you never take note of what you have done right, you deprive yourself of positive feedback that helps offset negative thoughts.

- **Examples of Small Steps:**
    - Getting out of bed on time, even if it felt extra hard.
    - Opening a textbook and reading one page.
    - Writing one paragraph for an essay.
    - Sending one supportive message to a friend.

Each of these can be a victory on days when depression is heavy. Appreciating them helps keep you going.

---

17. Using Visual Reminders

Sometimes, looking at a board or paper that lists your goal can keep it at the front of your mind. Depression can cause forgetfulness or a hazy mental state, so a visual cue helps you remember what you are aiming for.

- **Sticky Notes:** Place them on your mirror, desk, or notebook with small goals or uplifting phrases.
- **Posters or Printouts:** If you have a motivational quote or image that resonates with you, hang it where you see it daily.
- **Phone Alerts:** Set gentle reminders for breaks or micro-goals. Make sure they are not too intrusive; you do not want a dozen notifications that feel like nagging.

These reminders reinforce your intentions even when your mind tries to slip back into negative loops.

18. Combining Routine Goals with Variety

Routines can be soothing for someone with depression, providing stability. At the same time, too much sameness might dull your motivation. Mixing predictable elements with occasional new tasks can keep life from feeling stale.

- **Routines:** Maybe you always do 10 minutes of reading at 7 p.m. This consistency helps your mind and body expect certain activities at certain times.
- **New Activities:** Occasionally set a goal to try something different—like a new food recipe or a new corner of the library. Stepping out of your comfort zone in a safe way can break up monotony.

Balancing routine and novelty can maintain a delicate equilibrium where you feel both secure and stimulated.

---

19. Recognizing When Goals Need Professional Input

Sometimes, depression is severe enough that self-set goals become too challenging to pursue on your own. If you find that you constantly fail to start even simple tasks, feel extreme hopelessness, or have thoughts of harming yourself, it is time to involve mental health professionals more deeply.

- **Therapists:** They can help you create structured goal plans that take your mental state into account, and they can provide coping strategies when negative thoughts arise.
- **Counselors at School:** A school counselor can help balance your academic and personal goals, possibly making adjustments in your workload.
- **Psychiatrists or Doctors:** If medication is part of your treatment, they can ensure it is working effectively so you have enough mental clarity and energy for your goals.

Reaching out is not a sign of failure but a wise step to gather the support you need.

Chapter 17: Activities That Can Boost Mood

Daily life can sometimes feel dull or stressful, especially when you are dealing with depression. But there are activities you can explore that may lift your spirits, even if only by a small amount. While these ideas are not a magical fix for serious sadness, they can offer pleasant moments or serve as part of a broader strategy for feeling better. In this chapter, we will look at different mood-boosting activities, explaining why they might help, and how to get started even if you feel low on energy or motivation.

---

1. Why Activities Matter for Mood

When you feel down, your world can shrink. You might do the bare minimum—attending school (if you can), maybe doing a chore or two—then spend the rest of your time lying in bed or scrolling on your phone. While rest can be important, doing nothing day after day often leads to deeper hopelessness. Activities, especially ones that spark curiosity or enjoyment, can interrupt negative thought patterns and reintroduce small moments of satisfaction.

- **Positive Distraction:** Engaging in something fun or interesting can refocus your thoughts, even briefly, away from sadness or worries.
- **Sense of Achievement:** Completing a small project—like drawing a simple sketch or baking cookies—can bring a feeling of success.
- **Physical Benefits:** Activities that involve moving your body can lower tension, improve sleep, and sometimes help balance mood-related chemicals in the brain.
- **Social Connection:** Many activities can be done with others, which can reduce feelings of isolation.

You do not need to have huge bursts of enthusiasm to begin. Often, the action of doing an activity—however mildly you start—can itself spark a slight lift in mood.

---

2. Exploring Arts and Crafts

Creative pursuits like drawing, painting, or crafting can be a gentle way to express emotions without finding the "perfect words." You do not have to be a skilled artist to benefit from this. The process of creating can be soothing, helping you focus on colors, shapes, or textures rather than stressful thoughts.

1. **Drawing or Sketching:** You can start with simple doodles or basic lines. Some people find it relaxing to fill a page with repetitive patterns.
2. **Coloring Books:** These have become popular among teens and adults alike. Coloring within outlines can be calming and does not require complex skills.
3. **Collage Making:** Gather old magazines or photos and cut out images that catch your eye. Arrange them on paper in a way that feels interesting to you.
4. **Clay or Model Crafting:** Soft clay can be shaped into small figures or random objects. The tactile nature of clay can be grounding.
5. **Embroidery or Sewing:** Learning simple stitches can be surprisingly satisfying. Even if you just sew a heart shape onto a piece of cloth, it can feel like an achievement.

Why It Helps: Art can serve as an outlet for emotions, especially when talking feels too hard. Plus, seeing a final product—even if small—can nurture a sense of completion. If you want to share your creations, you might trade drawings with friends or post pictures online in supportive art communities.

---

3. Connecting with Nature

Spending time outdoors can bring a sense of calm. Even if you live in a city, you can look for small pockets of green—like a park, community garden, or tree-lined street. Nature can refresh you by appealing to your senses: the feel of a breeze, the sound of leaves rustling, or the sight of sunlight through branches.

1. **Walks in the Park:** A short, slow-paced stroll can help clear your head and get gentle exercise.
2. **Outdoor Observations:** Bring a small notebook and jot down any interesting birds, flowers, or cloud shapes you notice. Focusing on natural details can shift your thoughts away from internal worries.

3. **Picnics or Outdoor Reading:** If the weather is decent, take a snack or a book outside. Even half an hour in natural light can be uplifting.
4. **Gardening (If Possible):** Tending to plants—watering them, removing weeds—provides a sense of responsibility and small achievements as you see growth over time. If you do not have a yard, some herbs can grow on a windowsill.
5. **Neighborhood Exploration:** If there is a safe area near you, explore small paths, notice local trees, or watch how the sunlight changes in the late afternoon.

Why It Helps: Research shows that time in nature can reduce stress and boost positive feelings. If you cannot travel far, even sitting on a porch, balcony, or near an open window might offer some of these benefits.

---

4. Simple Body Movement

Exercise does not have to be intense. Gentle movement can sometimes lift your energy levels and release mood-supporting chemicals in your brain (like endorphins). If the thought of a long gym session feels overwhelming, consider smaller steps.

1. **Yoga or Stretching:** Basic yoga poses or stretches help you tune into your body. Many free videos show beginners' routines.
2. **Dance in Your Room:** Put on music you enjoy and move however you like. There is no need to follow set steps; just let the rhythm guide you.
3. **Short Walks or Easy Jog:** If jogging is too intense, a brisk walk might be enough to get your heart rate up. You can track distance or time to see small improvements.
4. **Light Sports with Friends:** A casual game of basketball or badminton can combine movement with social connection.
5. **Online Exercise Classes:** Some are specifically designed for beginners or for people with low energy. They might only last 10–15 minutes but can still help.

Why It Helps: Physical activity can break up the day and provide a reset for your mind. Even a small routine—like 10 minutes of stretching upon waking—can become a bright spot.

5. Trying Out Music

Music can influence emotions in powerful ways. Listening to songs you like, singing along (even quietly in your room), or learning a simple instrument can all shift mood in a positive direction.

1. **Curate Playlists:** Create playlists for different moods—one for calm, one for feeling more upbeat.
2. **Learn Basic Instrumental Skills:** You might pick up an inexpensive keyboard or guitar and watch beginner lessons online. Even learning a few chords can be rewarding.
3. **Sing or Hum:** Singing softly, even if you do not think you have a "good voice," can release tension. It can also regulate breathing.
4. **Music Appreciation:** Some teens find new genres or artists to explore, which can spark curiosity and excitement.
5. **Share Music with Friends:** Recommend songs to each other. This builds small social bridges and can help you feel connected.

Why It Helps: Music can validate how you feel or guide you toward a different mood. If you are sad, a gentle, reassuring song might comfort you. If you are low on energy, an upbeat tune might motivate you to move or try something else.

---

6. Small Acts of Kindness or Volunteering

It might sound odd to focus on helping others when you are the one feeling depressed. However, doing small acts of kindness can remind you that you can still make a positive difference in someone's day. This can fight the feeling of worthlessness or pointlessness.

1. **Compliment Someone Sincerely:** Whether online or in person, a genuine compliment can brighten both your day and theirs.
2. **Help a Younger Sibling or Neighbor:** Maybe assist with a simple chore, help them study, or keep them company in a safe way.
3. **Volunteer (If Possible):** Some organizations might allow short-term help, like sorting donations at a local drive. Even online volunteer tasks—like writing letters to seniors—can be meaningful.
4. **Creative Giving:** Make a small card for a friend, bake cookies for a neighbor, or send a kind message to someone who seems lonely.

Why It Helps: Acts of kindness often create a sense of purpose. You might realize, "I still have something to offer." This can gently push back against negative beliefs that come with depression.

---

7. Pet or Animal Interaction

Being around animals—if you like them—can be calming and uplifting. Not everyone has a pet, but there may be ways to interact with animals in safe environments.

1. **Play with a Pet:** If you have a cat or dog, spending time stroking or playing fetch can lower stress.
2. **Offer to Walk a Neighbor's Dog:** If you do not have your own pet but know someone who needs help, this could be a useful arrangement for both sides.
3. **Visit an Animal Shelter:** Some shelters welcome volunteers to help socialize cats or walk dogs. Even short visits might be possible.
4. **Watch Animals Online:** If you cannot be around real animals, cute or funny videos of pets can still bring a small smile.

Why It Helps: Animal companionship has been linked to reduced anxiety and lower blood pressure. Pets offer non-judgmental company, which can ease feelings of loneliness.

---

8. Exploring Hobbies or Interests

Hobbies can be short bursts of fun that remind you there is more to life than just sadness or stress. Try to think of things you used to like or that you have always been curious about.

1. **Reading or Listening to Audiobooks:** This can transport you to different worlds or let you learn about new topics.
2. **Puzzles and Brain Games:** Crosswords, word puzzles, or strategy games can give your mind a constructive challenge.
3. **Cooking or Baking:** Experiment with simple recipes. The act of measuring ingredients and following steps can absorb your attention. You might also enjoy the final product.

4. **Photography:** Even a phone camera can help you capture interesting angles, colors, or moments in daily life.
5. **Collecting:** Some people collect stickers, postcards, or small figures. Having a collection to grow and organize can be motivating.

Why It Helps: Engaging in an enjoyable hobby can produce small dopamine "rewards" in the brain, countering some of the chemistry of depression. It also gives you something to look forward to, even if it is just a few minutes each day.

---

9. Mindful Practices

Mindfulness involves paying attention to the present moment without judging it. This can be done through meditation, breathing exercises, or simply noticing your surroundings carefully. While mindfulness might seem challenging if you have racing thoughts, even short sessions can create pockets of calm.

1. **Basic Breathing Exercise:** Sit comfortably, inhale slowly through your nose for a count of four, hold for four, then exhale through your mouth for four. Repeat a few times.
2. **Body Scan Meditation:** Close your eyes and mentally check each part of your body from head to toe, noticing tension or sensations.
3. **Mindful Eating:** When you have a snack, focus on the taste, texture, and smell instead of multitasking or scrolling on your phone.
4. **Guided Videos or Apps:** Some apps offer free mindful sessions geared toward teens, helping you learn step by step.

Why It Helps: By anchoring your mind in the present, mindfulness can reduce the power of repetitive negative thoughts about the past or future. It takes practice, but many find even brief mindful breaks helpful over time.

---

10. Writing and Journaling

Putting words on paper can bring clarity. You do not need to show what you write to anyone. It can be purely for you, a place to express messy emotions or track daily ups and downs.

1. **Free Writing:** Set a timer for 5 or 10 minutes and write whatever crosses your mind, even if it is random or negative. This can be a mental "dump" to clear your head.
2. **Gratitude Notes:** Some find it grounding to write down one or two things they appreciated about the day, like a tasty meal or a funny meme that made them laugh.
3. **Poetry or Short Stories:** If you enjoy being creative, you can transform feelings into poems or fictional narratives.
4. **Lists of Observations:** You might list how you felt at different times of the day, noticing patterns like when sadness seems stronger or weaker.

Why It Helps: Journaling can make intangible feelings more tangible. Once you see words on paper, it can be easier to process or reflect on them, and you might identify patterns or triggers that contribute to your sadness.

---

11. Playing Games

Games—whether video games, board games, or card games—can supply a bit of fun and distraction. Socially, playing games with friends or family can build connections, but even solo gaming can provide a small mental break.

1. **Video Games:** If you choose story-driven or puzzle-focused games, they can immerse you in another world for a short time. Be mindful not to overdo it or use games as your only coping method.
2. **Board or Card Games with Friends:** A simple round of a classic card game might involve laughter or friendly competition, relieving tension.
3. **Online Multiplayer Games:** They can connect you with people worldwide. Aim for positive communities rather than toxic environments.

Why It Helps: Games can help you focus on objectives and strategies, leaving less room for negative thoughts. They also offer mini-goals and achievements that may give small boosts of satisfaction.

---

12. Planning Small Outings or "Mini Adventures"

If you can, scheduling a short trip out of your usual environment can bring excitement and break monotony. These do not have to be expensive or far away.

1. **Local Museum or Community Event:** If there is a free or low-cost exhibit, exploring it might spark curiosity.
2. **Trying a New Café:** If possible, visit a place you have never been. Even ordering a new flavor of drink can feel like a tiny adventure.
3. **Library Visit:** Libraries often have not just books, but also community boards for local events. Browsing shelves can inspire you with new topics.
4. **Walking a Different Route:** Instead of your usual path, choose a different street or park. Notice how it feels to see new surroundings.

Why It Helps: Novel experiences shake up the routine. You may find small surprises or interesting details that remind you life has variety beyond your current struggles.

---

13. Creating a Comfort Space at Home

Sometimes, you cannot go out, or you do not feel up to it. In such cases, you can design a cozy corner in your room or elsewhere in the house where you can relax or enjoy a favorite activity.

1. **Blankets and Pillows:** Soft textures can be soothing.
2. **Soft Lighting:** Harsh lights can be unpleasant. A soft lamp or string lights might create a calmer atmosphere.
3. **Favorite Scent (If Safe):** A mild scented candle or essential oil diffuser can add a comforting smell, like lavender or vanilla (make sure it is allowed and safe in your home).
4. **Music or White Noise:** Some people like gentle music, others prefer nature sounds or plain white noise to relax.
5. **Meaningful Objects:** You might place a few items that remind you of positive memories, such as photos, letters, or small souvenirs.

Why It Helps: Having a designated spot where you feel safe and supported can be a retreat when sadness intensifies. You can go there to read, journal, or just breathe in a calmer environment.

14. Joining Local or Online Clubs

If you have the energy to reach out, joining a club—either in school or online—can provide a sense of belonging and give you a reason to do something on a regular schedule.

1. **School Clubs:** Whether it is art, chess, drama, or a cultural club, it can be a structured way to meet people and do activities together.
2. **Online Communities:** Look for forums or social media groups dedicated to interests like writing, coding, crafts, or a favorite show. Aim for supportive, positive spaces.
3. **Community Classes:** Some areas offer free or low-cost classes for teens in dance, ceramics, or cooking. Attending can broaden your skills and social circle.

Why It Helps: Being part of a group can remind you that you are not alone. Shared interests can spark conversation topics that do not revolve around sadness. Even reading others' posts in an online community can feel validating.

---

15. Setting Micro-Challenges

A "micro-challenge" is a tiny, bite-sized goal. For example, "I will learn how to fold an origami crane today" or "I will organize one small section of my desk." These challenges are easy to start and finish quickly.

- **Examples:**
    - Fold 10 paper cranes in a week.
    - Memorize a short poem or quote.
    - Clean out one drawer in your room.
    - Try a new hairstyle or learn a simple magic trick.

Why It Helps: Completing a micro-challenge provides a small sense of accomplishment. It builds momentum that can carry over to bigger tasks or simply offer a refreshing change of pace.

16. Exploring Personal Style and Self-Expression

Changing how you present yourself can sometimes shift how you feel inside. This is not about pleasing others, but about experimenting with your own preferences and identity.

1. **Try Out a Different Clothing Combination:** If you usually wear dark colors, add a bright scarf or accessory. Or if you never wear hats, see what happens when you do.
2. **Temporary Hair Experiments:** If allowed at home/school, use washable hair color or experiment with a different styling technique.
3. **Make a Mood Board of Styles:** Cut out pictures from magazines or save images online that represent looks you find interesting.
4. **Subtle Changes in Routine:** Switching from glasses to contacts (if you use them), or wearing a small piece of jewelry that you typically keep hidden, might bring novelty.

Why It Helps: Self-expression can reinforce that you have some control over your life. Trying new looks can challenge negative feelings about yourself by revealing different ways you can appear or feel.

---

17. Digital Detox Sessions

Constant screen time, especially if you tend to compare yourself to others on social media, can strain your mood. Planning short "digital detox" periods might give your mind a break.

1. **Set a Timer for Offline Time:** For instance, no phone usage for 30 minutes before bed or after waking up.
2. **Replace Screen Time with an Alternative:** If you usually scroll through apps for an hour, try filling that slot with a quiet activity like doodling or tidying up a part of your room.
3. **Limit Notifications:** Turn off or reduce alerts, so you are not constantly pulled back to your phone.
4. **Use Apps that Track Screen Use:** Seeing how many hours you spend on your phone might motivate you to cut back gradually.

Why It Helps: Constant online engagement can fuel anxious or depressed thoughts, especially if you see upsetting news or negative posts. Brief breaks can clear your head, letting you do something more nurturing.

---

18. Keeping a Mood Log

To see what truly helps or worsens your mood, you can keep track of activities and how you feel after trying them. This does not need to be complicated.

1. **Daily Mood Rating:** Rate your mood from 1 to 10 each day. Next to it, note major events or activities.
2. **Short Comments:** Write a quick sentence like "Went for a walk—felt a bit better afterward" or "Argued with a sibling—felt worse."
3. **Look for Patterns:** Over a week or two, you might see that certain activities consistently boost your mood slightly, while others might have the opposite effect.

Why It Helps: This objective record can guide you to choose more helpful activities in the future and avoid repeating what seems to intensify low feelings. It also shows that your mood can vary, which is a reminder that you are not stuck in one emotional state forever.

---

19. Pairing Up with a "Mood Buddy"

A "mood buddy" is a friend or relative who also wants to improve or maintain their mental well-being. You can support each other by trying a new activity at the same time or comparing notes on how you felt.

- **Co-Work or Co-Study Sessions:** If one of your goals is to be productive, working alongside someone—even virtually—can help. You can pause occasionally to stretch or chat.
- **Shared Challenges:** You might both agree to practice a new craft or test a simple recipe, then talk about how it went.
- **Checking In Regularly:** Send a message like, "How are you doing today? Did you try our planned activity?" This accountability can be gently motivating.

Why It Helps: Knowing someone else is also aiming to boost their mood can reduce isolation. You can share small successes and reassure each other during tough moments.

---

20. Staying Realistic About Mood Boosting

Not every activity will magically transform your mood, and that is okay. You might only feel a tiny spark of relief or enjoyment. On some days, you might try something and still feel quite sad. The key is to see these activities as part of a bigger picture—gradually adding small rays of light into your life rather than an instant cure.

- **Accepting Mild Improvements:** If an activity lightens your mood from a very low place to just a slightly less low place, that is still progress.
- **Experimenting Without Judgment:** If painting did not help much, maybe music will. If yoga felt awkward, try short walks instead. Different approaches suit different people.
- **Being Patient:** Depression often affects motivation. It might take multiple attempts before you notice any consistent benefit.
- **Combining Approaches:** Pairing these activities with therapy, possible medication, and a supportive environment can create a stronger foundation for improvement.

Remember that you do not need to force yourself to do all these suggestions at once. Pick one or two that seem mildly interesting or least draining. Even if you can only manage a few minutes a day, that small effort can be a step forward. Over time, collecting these little moments of positive engagement can chip away at the heaviness of depression, giving you more options to handle daily challenges.

Chapter 18: Learning from Positive Examples

Looking to others for inspiration can be a powerful way to see what is possible. While no one's situation matches yours exactly, hearing about people who have faced tough times and found ways to cope can offer a spark of hope. Positive examples are not only about famous historical figures or celebrities; they can also include people in your community, classmates, teachers, relatives, or friends who have navigated sadness or struggled with anxiety yet managed to keep going. This chapter will explore how to find and learn from role models, real or fictional, and how to adapt their lessons to your own life without feeling pressured to become a copy of them.

---

1. Why Role Models Can Help

Depression often clouds your view of what is possible. You might assume, "My situation is hopeless; nothing works." When you see or hear about someone who has been through difficulties but still found a path forward, it challenges that assumption. It does not mean you must replicate their life, but it can remind you that improvement or resilience is feasible.

- **Encouragement:** Realizing someone else has overcome a similar issue can spark a bit of determination in you.
- **Practical Tips:** Role models sometimes share methods or choices they made. Even if your life is different, some of their strategies might be adaptable.
- **Connection:** Knowing you are not alone in struggling can reduce shame. Humans have faced mental health issues for centuries, and many have navigated them successfully.

---

2. Identifying Positive Figures in Everyday Life

Celebrities or historical icons are one source of inspiration, but everyday people around you might offer more personal and relatable examples.

1. **Friends or Peers:** Maybe a classmate used to be very anxious and has found healthier ways to cope. They could share how they started opening up to a counselor or joined a supportive group.
2. **Family Members:** An older cousin might have gone through a rocky phase in their teen years and is now calmer. A parent or guardian might have experienced depression themselves at some point.
3. **Teachers or Coaches:** Sometimes adults at school can share their own stories of challenges. If they are open about it, you might realize they overcame stumbling blocks you are facing now.
4. **Community Leaders or Neighbors:** A neighbor might have faced life difficulties—like losing a job or dealing with an illness—yet remained kind, helpful, and steady. Observing how they handle stress can be informative.

Why It Helps: Seeing real people you know who have grown through adversity can be more convincing than reading about celebrities who live in very different circumstances.

---

3. Gathering Inspiration from Well-Known People

Historically, many famous figures—scientists, artists, athletes—have battled mood disorders, anxiety, or other setbacks. While you cannot replicate their entire lives, bits of their stories might provide hope or ideas.

1. **Authors with Mental Health Struggles:** Some well-known writers openly discussed depression in their journals or memoirs. Learning how they continued to create despite dark times can be motivating if you like writing.
2. **Artists Who Overcame Barriers:** Painters or musicians who used their craft to process sorrow could show that channeling feelings into art is possible.
3. **Athletes Who Faced Injuries or Emotional Challenges:** Many star athletes had periods of self-doubt or major setbacks but came back with consistent training and support.
4. **Scientists or Inventors with Persistent Efforts:** Some invented breakthroughs after numerous failures. While not always about mental health, their determination can remind you that repeated tries can lead to progress.

Why It Helps: It places your struggles in context. Seeing that even admired figures had hard times but found ways to persist can combat the idea that you have no chance.

4. Reading or Watching Recovery Stories

A variety of books, articles, or documentary videos feature people sharing their journeys through depression or related challenges. These can be real-life stories or fictional ones that mirror aspects of real struggles.

- **Memoirs of People Who Faced Depression:** They might detail how they felt at their lowest and what steps led to improvement.
- **Online Articles or Blogs:** Sometimes individuals blog about coping strategies or daily ups and downs. Look for reputable sources, especially if they provide helpful, balanced perspectives.
- **Documentaries or Interviews:** Watching someone speak about their depression and how they managed it can be more emotionally direct than reading words on a page.
- **Fictional Stories with Realistic Struggles:** Certain novels or films depict characters dealing with sadness in a nuanced way. These can reflect real feelings and possible paths to healing.

Why It Helps: Seeing the entire arc of someone's struggle, not just the result, can normalize the bumpy path. It can also remind you that relapses or setbacks do not mean permanent failure.

5. Recognizing That No One Is Perfect

When looking up to someone, there is a risk of idolizing them. You might think they always have it together, which can make you feel worse about your own mistakes or ongoing troubles. Remember that role models are human. They have flaws, make errors, and have rough days. The valuable lesson is not that they are perfect, but that they keep going despite imperfection.

1. **Accepting Imperfections in Role Models:** Notice how they handle slip-ups. Do they show resilience by learning from them? That approach might be what you want to emulate, rather than aiming for zero mistakes.

2. **Avoiding Harsh Comparison:** Instead of saying, "They overcame sadness in a year; why can't I?" use their progress to encourage yourself, not to criticize your own pace.
3. **Learning Only What Applies:** If a role model's life is very different, pick the elements that resonate with you. You do not have to adopt every part of their routine or beliefs.

Why It Helps: Realizing your heroes have flaws reminds you that you do not need to be flawless to see improvement in your own mental health.

6. Adapting Ideas to Your Own Life

A role model might swear by morning workouts or journaling three pages every night, but what if your energy is too low in the morning, or writing three pages seems impossible? You can adjust these ideas to fit your current reality.

- **Start Smaller:** If they do a 30-minute workout daily, try five or ten minutes, a couple of times a week.
- **Change the Format:** If they journal every night, maybe you record a short voice note instead, or doodle one sketch if writing feels tough.
- **Combine with Your Interests:** If they practice mindfulness but you prefer music, maybe do a brief mindful listening exercise to your favorite calming track.
- **Drop What Does Not Click:** Not every strategy will work for you. That is normal. Let go of methods that cause extra stress or do not resonate.

Why It Helps: By customizing, you prevent frustration that arises from copying someone else exactly. You build your own pattern of coping that aligns with your needs.

7. Learning from Positive Peer Groups

Beyond individual role models, groups or communities that foster encouragement can be equally powerful. A supportive environment can show you multiple examples of resilience and ways to handle setbacks.

1. **Support Groups:** Some organizations or community centers hold teen support group sessions. Listening to peers discuss their experiences can offer real-life coping tactics.
2. **Clubs with Shared Interests:** Being around others who share your passions can give you a sense of belonging. Observing how they face personal problems might give you tips.
3. **Online Communities:** Look for groups focused on mental well-being or on a particular hobby. Interacting in forums can expose you to success stories and gentle support.
4. **Class Projects or Team Activities:** Working together on a group project can reveal classmates who have good ways of dealing with stress—like dividing tasks fairly or staying calm under deadlines.

Why It Helps: Peer groups can normalize discussions about feelings. You might pick up coping ideas from multiple sources, weaving together an approach that suits you.

---

8. Fictional Characters as Inspiration

Sometimes fictional heroes or protagonists undergo emotional battles that reflect real-life challenges. Even if their world is full of fantasy elements, their internal struggles can be relatable.

1. **Books or Comics:** Characters who start out insecure but grow braver or kinder can encourage you to persist in your own journey.
2. **Movies or Shows:** Notice how characters confront dilemmas, gather support from friends, or learn from failures.
3. **Relatable Themes:** Maybe a show features a teen balancing school stress, family drama, and personal doubts. Observing how they handle these might spark ideas or at least help you feel less alone.

Why It Helps: Fiction can deliver messages about hope, friendship, and perseverance in a more symbolic or entertaining way. You might find it easier to absorb these lessons without feeling lectured.

---

9. Short Quotes or Affirmations

Some people find motivation in short, memorable lines. These can come from well-known individuals or from personal phrases that capture a piece of encouragement. You could post them on a bulletin board, write them on sticky notes, or keep them in your phone.

- **Examples of Positive Quotes:**
    - "This too shall pass."
    - "Small steps every day."
    - "I am doing the best I can with what I have today."
    - "Struggle means I have not given up."

Why It Helps: A brief phrase can act as a mental nudge when negative thoughts take over. They are not cures, but can disrupt a cascade of unhelpful thinking, reminding you that others have faced difficulties and kept going.

---

10. Looking at How Others Manage Self-Care

Sometimes you might observe that a friend or family member is less anxious or handles stress better. If appropriate, you could ask what routines or self-care methods they use. People are often glad to share.

1. **Ask About Sleep Routines:** If you know someone who wakes up feeling more rested, they might have bedtime habits (like no phone after 9 p.m.) that you can try.
2. **Ask About Meal Choices:** A person who always seems to have balanced energy might plan their meals and snacks to avoid big energy drops.
3. **Ask About Emotional Coping:** Perhaps they do a quick breathing exercise when overwhelmed, or they call a friend.
4. **Respect Boundaries:** Not everyone will want to open up about personal tactics, but many will appreciate that you value their example.

Why It Helps: Adopting or adapting a small part of someone's self-care plan can refine your own approach, creating better daily habits.

---

11. Observing Problem-Solving Approaches

People who navigate difficulties effectively often have strategies to tackle problems step by step. If you see someone calmly handle conflicts or solve issues, notice how they do it.

- **Breaking Problems Down:** They might identify one aspect of the situation at a time instead of feeling paralyzed by the whole.
- **Seeking Help:** They may ask for advice, dividing tasks with friends or using resources.
- **Learning from Mistakes:** If a plan fails, they do not call themselves a failure; they try a different angle.

Why It Helps: It is easy to get stuck in negative thought loops when depressed. Seeing someone systematically address issues can remind you that methodical approaches might help you handle challenges, too.

---

12. Gathering Insights from Counselors or Mentors

A school counselor, teacher, or mental health mentor might have seen many students overcome obstacles. They can share examples (while respecting privacy) of teens who turned corners in their emotional well-being.

1. **Success Stories (in General Terms):** A counselor might say, "I had a student who felt hopeless about grades, but we made a schedule, and eventually they raised them enough to graduate on time."
2. **Practical Steps Learned:** They could show how that teen managed time or balanced rest and study.
3. **Mentor-Apprentice Approach:** Sometimes a mentor can guide you step by step in a skill, whether it is academic or emotional self-regulation.

Why It Helps: Hearing about common patterns of improvement can reduce the feeling that you are uniquely stuck. Counselors also often provide realistic perspectives on how change can be gradual.

13. Avoiding Toxic Comparisons

While looking at others can be helpful, you must be careful not to fall into harmful comparisons. If you constantly think, "They got better faster," or "They have more friends, so I'll never succeed," you might deepen your sadness.

- **Set Personal Benchmarks:** Measure your progress against where you were a few weeks or months ago, not against someone else's timeline.
- **Seek Inspiration, Not Pressure:** If a friend overcame a challenge, focus on the positive possibility for you rather than turning it into "They are better, so I am worse."
- **Acknowledge Different Circumstances:** Everyone's background, support network, and health is different. What took them one month might take you longer, or vice versa.

Why It Helps: Balanced comparison can keep you open to learning, while negative comparison can block the benefits of a role model's story.

---

14. Creating a Personal Inspiration Board or File

Collect photos, quotes, short stories, or achievements that remind you of hope. This can be digital (a folder on your phone) or physical (a corkboard in your room).

1. **Include People You Admire:** Print out a quote from your favorite athlete or a snapshot of a friend who overcame challenges.
2. **Highlight Your Own Wins:** Sometimes a small certificate, a note from a friend, or a personal best in a game can go here. You do not have to share it publicly—it is for you to see.
3. **Refresh It Over Time:** As you grow, remove items that no longer resonate and add new ones that spark motivation.

Why It Helps: This board or file can be a quick reference when you feel down. A few seconds of scanning can remind you of strengths, resilience, and supportive figures.

---

15. Conversations with Trusted People

Sometimes, the best way to learn from someone is a simple chat. If you have a friend, relative, or teacher who has experience with mental health, you could ask if they are comfortable discussing it.

- **Sample Questions:**
    - "How did you handle days when you really did not want to get out of bed?"
    - "What kind of things helped you keep going, even when it felt pointless?"
    - "Did you ever feel like giving up? How did you move past that feeling?"
- **Listen Attentively:** Let them speak without interruption. They might share a golden piece of advice or a personal story that resonates deeply.

Why It Helps: Personal stories can be far more detailed and nuanced than general advice. They also allow you to ask follow-up questions, clarifying how you might adapt their ideas.

---

16. Learning from People Who Support Others

Observing those who help friends or family with mental health concerns can also teach you supportive strategies. For instance, you might notice how a family member calmly reassures someone during a panic attack, or how a friend organizes study sessions for a stressed classmate.

- **Communication Cues:** Look at how they speak—gently but firmly, perhaps, or how they show empathy without judgment.
- **Encouraging Boundaries:** Good supporters respect personal limits. They help but do not force solutions.
- **Seeing Care in Action:** This can inspire you to accept help more readily or to offer the same type of thoughtful gestures to yourself or others.

Why It Helps: Witnessing care fosters the idea that your environment can be supportive. You might replicate those gestures in your own self-talk or while assisting a peer.

17. Handling Disappointment If a Role Model Falls Short

Sometimes role models can disappoint us. A celebrity might say something hurtful, or a friend might behave in ways that break your trust. This does not erase the helpful insights you gained, but it requires a shift in perspective.

- **Separate Their Actions from Their Tips:** If their ideas or methods were helpful, you do not need to discard them just because they made a mistake.
- **Recall Human Flaws:** Even good people make unwise choices. You can still value parts of their example while rejecting behaviors that hurt or upset you.
- **Look for Other Sources of Inspiration:** It is good to have multiple role models, so you are not dependent on just one person's image.

Why It Helps: Disappointment is a normal part of life. Learning to navigate it without rejecting all the positives you once gained from that person can keep you balanced.

---

18. Small Exercises to Use Role Models Constructively

If you want a structured way to learn from others, try these mini-exercises:

1. **Role Model Reflection:** Write about someone you admire, focusing on the difficulties they overcame. List any strategies you could try.
2. **Weekly Example Check:** Each week, look for one example in your real life or online of someone handling adversity well. Note what you liked about it.
3. **Adapt One Strategy:** Pick one action they took. Apply it in your own scale. For example, if they took morning walks, maybe you do a short walk around the block once a week to start.
4. **Compare Old and New You:** After a month, reflect on whether this new habit helped or if you prefer to try something else next.

Why It Helps: These steps bring structure to the process of learning from examples, ensuring you apply what you observe instead of just admiring it from a distance.

19. Balancing Inspiration with Personal Responsibility

Role models can guide and encourage, but ultimately, you control your own life decisions. It might be tempting to think, "I'll just do what they did," but remember that your situation, personality, and environment matter.

- **You Still Matter in the Equation:** Their story is not your story. Borrow tactics that fit, but be ready to modify them.
- **Progress Takes Time:** If your role model seems to have quickly bounced back, they might have had past experiences or resources you do not see. Your timeline can be slower or different.
- **Combine Various Influences:** You could learn a coping skill from a local friend, glean a motivational quote from an athlete, and pick up a scheduling trick from a teacher. Creating your own blend might be most helpful.

Why It Helps: This mindset prevents frustration or self-blame. You remain open to learning but do not expect an exact copy-and-paste solution for your depression.

20. Keeping Perspective

It is easy for depression to trick you into believing you are the only one who struggles. Positive examples—whether from everyday people, historical figures, or fictional heroes—remind you that humans share common experiences of hardship and growth. Learning from their paths can reduce isolation and inspire you to try small experiments in your own life.

As you gather role models' ideas, remain patient with yourself. You might attempt something that worked wonders for them, only to feel little difference at first. That does not mean you will never find relief. Keep an open mind, stay flexible, and build a personal support network that allows you to gather bits of wisdom from multiple sources. Over time, you can piece together your own approach, shaped by what you have learned from others yet firmly guided by your unique needs.

Chapter 19: Keeping Up Long-Term Well-Being

Reaching a point where depression feels more manageable can bring relief and a sense that life might become brighter. However, maintaining well-being over time can be a challenge in itself. You might notice mood dips return during busy weeks, or triggers from your past re-emerge. Keeping up good habits and healthy thinking is not a one-time act, but an ongoing process. This chapter will discuss ways to maintain your mental health gains and stay proactive, even when life throws curveballs. We will also address warning signs that might suggest you need extra support again, because lapses do not mean failure; they are simply reminders to refocus on what helps you thrive.

1. Recognizing the Shifting Nature of Mood

Depression is often not a neat, one-time phase that disappears forever. Some people find they have periods of feeling much better, then face low spells again. This is normal. There are many factors—like hormones, school stress, family events, or even changes in weather—that can influence mood shifts. A key step is knowing that an occasional dip does not undo all progress. It may feel discouraging, but it can also remind you to revisit your coping strategies.

1. **Accepting Ebb and Flow:** Moods can naturally shift. You might wake up feeling great and feel sluggish by evening, or vice versa. Learning to observe these changes without panicking can help you respond calmly.
2. **Evaluating Patterns:** If you see that low phases appear during certain times—like exam weeks—plan ahead. Set up extra self-care or supportive activities in those seasons.
3. **Using Tools You Have Practiced:** The methods you learned in earlier chapters—mindfulness, small goals, reaching out to a trusted friend—still work. Even if it feels repetitive, returning to them can prevent a temporary slide from becoming a major setback.

Why It Matters: Understanding that depression's ups and downs might recur prevents you from feeling blindsided or defeated. It allows you to maintain a sense of control and readiness.

2. Keeping a Supportive Daily Routine

Routines can act like the scaffolding that keeps your day organized. When you have regular sleeping hours, meal times, and planned activities, you reduce chaotic stretches where negative thoughts can intensify. This does not mean your life must be rigid, but a flexible structure can balance a teen's busy schedule and emotional needs.

1. **Consistent Sleep Patterns:** Aim for a regular bedtime, plus or minus 30 minutes. Waking up around the same time daily can help regulate your body's internal clock.
2. **Scheduled Meals and Snacks:** Skipping meals can lead to energy dips and irritability. Even simple breakfasts—like fruit or toast—can set the tone for better concentration.
3. **Time for Homework, Time for Rest:** Break academic tasks into chunks, scheduling short breaks to prevent burnout.
4. **Device-Free Intervals:** Consider keeping your phone off for a certain time each day, maybe during meals or before bed, to reduce overstimulation.
5. **Incorporate Pleasure Activities:** This might be reading a favorite comic for 15 minutes or doing a quick craft. Knowing you have something fun planned can lift your mood during stressful parts of the day.

Why It Matters: A routine is not about perfection. It is about creating an environment where you can thrive more often than not. Even small improvements—like sleeping a bit earlier—can show results over weeks.

---

3. Building an Ongoing Self-Care Toolkit

Self-care is more than an occasional treat. It is an everyday approach to looking after your mind and body. While you might already have strategies, it helps to think of them as part of a toolkit: a set of resources you can pull from when stress rises or low mood creeps in.

1. **List the Tools:** You could write them down or store them in your phone. Include things like "take a 5-minute walk," "listen to uplifting music," or "text a supportive friend."

2. **Have Quick Options:** Some days, you will only have a few minutes between classes. If your toolkit has 1-minute breathing exercises or 2-minute stretches, you can use them anywhere.
3. **Include Larger Activities:** For weekends or breaks, you might want a bigger project—like painting or a day trip with family. Keep those ideas ready so you are not stuck idly scrolling on your phone.
4. **Refresh Periodically:** As you grow or your interests shift, your toolkit might need updates. If you stop enjoying coloring books, replace that with another soothing activity you find appealing.

Why It Matters: Having a tangible set of coping strategies takes the guesswork out of what to do when you feel overwhelmed. You will not need to think too hard in a crisis; you can just pick an item from your list.

---

4. Monitoring Your Digital Habits

In earlier chapters, we talked about limiting negative online content. Long-term well-being also depends on maintaining healthy boundaries with technology. It is easy for habits to slip—especially if you get busy or bored—and find yourself spending hours on social media again, possibly absorbing negativity or comparing yourself to others.

1. **Regular Check-Ins:** Every few weeks, evaluate how you are using devices. Is it starting to feel out of control? Are you seeing more negative posts than before?
2. **Adjust Settings:** If you notice certain apps trigger sadness or stress, remove them or reduce notifications. You can reinstall them later if your approach changes.
3. **Digital Break Challenges:** Try setting a goal: no social media after 8 p.m. for a week. See if your sleep improves or your mood feels steadier.
4. **Curate Content:** Follow accounts that uplift, inform, or entertain you in positive ways. Unfollow or mute accounts that fuel envy or negativity.

Why It Matters: Technology itself is not the enemy. But using it mindlessly or immersing yourself in harmful content can undo the emotional stability you have built.

5. Staying Active in Supportive Communities

Depression can slowly push you to isolate, even if you have improved. Over time, you might skip group activities or stop responding to messages. One key to ongoing wellness is maintaining connections with groups or friends who genuinely care about you.

1. **School Clubs or Teams:** If you joined a club or sports team that brought you some happiness, consider continuing with it or renewing membership each semester.
2. **Online Peer Support Circles:** Certain moderated online forums or group chats can keep you accountable and remind you that you are not alone.
3. **Community Volunteering:** If you ever found purpose in volunteering (like a soup kitchen or animal shelter), keep it in your routine. Even once a month can be meaningful.
4. **Religious or Spiritual Groups (If Relevant):** For those who practice a faith, staying connected to a supportive community can foster hope and fellowship.

Why It Matters: Isolation often creeps in when we stop tending to our social roots. Regular engagement with supportive circles can reinforce self-worth and stability.

---

6. Balancing Responsibilities and Relaxation

As you get older, you may take on more tasks—AP classes, part-time work, family chores. While achievement can boost self-esteem, it can also lead to overwhelm if not balanced. Keeping depression at bay means knowing when to step back and rest.

1. **Time Management Skills:** Use a planner or a simple digital calendar to avoid last-minute panic. Spreading tasks out can reduce stress spikes.
2. **Saying "No" Sometimes:** If you tend to overcommit, practice politely declining extra obligations. You cannot do everything, and that is okay.
3. **Scheduling Relaxation:** Rather than leaving rest to chance, block out a weekly hour just for yourself—no chores, no errands, just calm downtime.
4. **Identifying Warning Signs of Overload:** If you begin losing sleep or snapping at friends, that could signal you are juggling too much. Scale back before it triggers a deeper slump.

Why It Matters: A balanced lifestyle helps sustain mental health long-term. Overwork might bring short success, but eventually leads to exhaustion, which can feed depression.

---

7. Reassessing Goals and Adjusting Them

Goals help you progress, but they should evolve as you do. After months of working on personal challenges, you might find your ambitions have shifted. Periodically checking in on your goals ensures they remain relevant, enjoyable, and aligned with your current mood and growth.

1. **Monthly or Quarterly Reviews:** Look at what you aimed to do. Are these still important to you?
2. **Refine or Replace Goals:** If a goal feels stale, update it. For instance, if you wanted to run a mile and now you can, maybe aim for 1.5 miles, or switch to trying a new sport.
3. **Balance Ambition with Realism:** It is good to push yourself, but not to the point of unrealistic pressure. Keep a gentle challenge that fits your current energy level.

Why It Matters: Progress can stall when goals become outdated or when you no longer connect with them. Adjusting keeps your motivation fresh and supports consistent well-being.

---

8. Checking in with Yourself

Emotional self-awareness is a vital skill. Instead of letting feelings build until they explode, maintain a habit of internal check-ins. You can do this daily, weekly, or whenever you sense something is off.

1. **Ask Basic Questions:** "How am I feeling today?" "Is there anything troubling me?" "Am I neglecting any crucial self-care?"
2. **Use a Mood Scale:** Rate your day from 1 to 10, or use words (like "tense," "light," "okay"). Over time, see if you notice patterns or triggers.
3. **Be Honest:** If you realize you are struggling more than usual, do not brush it off. Name it. Then decide which coping or support method to use.

4. **Avoid Harsh Judgment:** Checking in is not about scolding yourself. It is about taking a compassionate view of your emotional state.

Why It Matters: Consistent awareness lets you catch small declines in mood before they escalate, giving you a chance to intervene early.

---

9. Knowing Your Triggers and Warning Signs

Long-term well-being involves recognizing situations, relationships, or thoughts that can push you back toward deeper sadness or negative behaviors. This is not about fearing triggers but about being prepared.

1. **Common Triggers:** It might be a certain family conflict, an anniversary of a tough event, or even a type of content on social media.
2. **Warning Signs:** These might include withdrawing from friends, appetite changes, trouble sleeping, or persistent negative self-talk.
3. **Response Plan:** If you identify you are nearing a negative zone, act. Use your coping toolkit, call a friend, or talk to a counselor.
4. **Adjusting Environments:** If a certain crowd is constantly belittling you, consider limiting contact. If a location stirs up painful memories, maybe go there with a supportive person until you feel safer.

Why It Matters: Being proactive about triggers prevents you from feeling powerless. You can face them with a plan rather than waiting for a crisis.

---

10. Maintaining Therapy or Counseling if It Helps

After feeling better for a while, some teens stop seeing their counselor or therapist. While you can certainly reduce or change therapy schedules, quitting too early might cut off a valuable resource. Regular check-ins—even if they are less frequent—can keep you on track.

1. **Discuss Timeline with Your Therapist:** If you are improving, you can talk about spacing sessions out. But do not vanish without a conversation.
2. **Booster Sessions:** Some people attend monthly or quarterly sessions to keep up strategies and handle new stressors.

3. **Alternatives if You Stop Therapy:** If therapy becomes too expensive or time-consuming, seek other support. That might be group counseling at school, free hotlines, or a school counselor.
4. **Revisit If You Struggle Again:** If you notice yourself sliding into deeper sadness, do not be afraid to go back to therapy. It is not a step backward; it is a wise move to maintain well-being.

Why It Matters: Mental health maintenance can be like physical health check-ups. Even when you feel stable, periodic professional input can catch early signs of trouble and offer fresh perspectives.

11. Staying Aware of Physical Health

Your physical condition and mental state are intertwined. Chronic illness, hormonal shifts, or simply not taking care of your body can undermine your emotional stability.

1. **Regular Check-Ups:** Visit a doctor if you have unexplained fatigue, pain, or changes in appetite. Sometimes physical issues mimic or worsen depression.
2. **Nutrition Basics:** You do not need a perfect diet, but balanced meals with vegetables, proteins, and whole grains can help stabilize mood.
3. **Exercise Routines:** Even short activities—like 20 minutes of moderate walking—have benefits for mood regulation.
4. **Screening for Vitamin Deficiencies:** Lack of certain vitamins (e.g., D, B12) can contribute to low mood or tiredness. A doctor can advise on tests or supplements if needed.

Why It Matters: Overlooking physical health can sabotage your best efforts at emotional well-being. Taking care of your body supports a more stable emotional foundation.

12. Practicing Relapse Prevention Techniques

Relapse prevention often refers to steps taken to avoid sliding back into harmful patterns, whether that is substance misuse or self-harm. But it can also apply to depression's more severe episodes. The idea is to have a plan when you sense warning signs.

1. **Identify Vulnerable Times:** For instance, the beginning of a new school year might bring anxiety, or holidays might trigger loneliness.
2. **List Early Symptoms:** Maybe you withdraw socially, skip homework, or skip meals. Recognizing these changes can be your signal to act.
3. **Create a Crisis Plan:** Write down who to call (a friend, parent, or hotline) if you feel overwhelmed. Keep coping methods and emergency numbers visible.
4. **Share with Trusted People:** Let them know what to watch for, so they can nudge you if they see those warning signs.

Why It Matters: Having a relapse prevention mindset means you do not wait until you are deeply in crisis. You intervene early, saving yourself from bigger setbacks.

---

13. Developing a Sense of Purpose

Some teens find that focusing on a meaningful pursuit makes them more resilient. Purpose does not mean solving huge world problems overnight; it might be as simple as caring for a pet, enjoying a creative hobby, or supporting a cause you believe in.

1. **Explore Interests:** Try different things—photography, volunteer programs, local clubs. If you find something that resonates, spend more time on it.
2. **Set Service-Related Goals:** Maybe pledge a few hours a month to a local organization or help younger students with homework. Feeling needed can boost self-esteem.
3. **Grow Hobbies into Passions:** If you love drawing, join an art challenge. If music energizes you, practice a bit more seriously or share songs with friends.
4. **Reflect on Personal Values:** Think about what you stand for—kindness, creativity, honesty. Aligning daily actions with these values can create a deeper sense of life direction.

Why It Matters: A sense of purpose often acts like a shield against recurring emptiness. It gives you something to look forward to, making negative thoughts a bit easier to manage.

14. Continuing to Learn About Mental Health

Mental health is a vast field, and new research or tools appear regularly. Staying informed can empower you and show you are proactive about your well-being.

1. **Reading Articles or Books:** Check reputable sources that discuss teen mental health, coping mechanisms, or personal stories.
2. **Following Mental Health Organizations Online:** Some post tips or share new strategies for stress management.
3. **Webinars or Workshops:** Occasionally, schools or local groups hold mental health awareness events. Attending can refresh your knowledge and help you meet others with similar goals.
4. **Asking Questions:** If something puzzles you, such as new therapy trends or mindfulness apps, do a bit of research or ask a counselor.

Why It Matters: Treat your mental well-being as an ongoing subject of learning. You can refine your skills, discover fresh methods, and stay prepared for new life stages.

---

15. Addressing Relationship Dynamics

Over time, your friendships and family connections may evolve. People grow, conflicts arise, or new relationships form. Keeping up long-term well-being involves navigating these changes with minimal harm to yourself.

1. **Communicate Boundaries:** If you need space or if certain jokes upset you, voice it. This can prevent misunderstandings from festering.
2. **Resolve Problems Early:** Avoid letting tensions build. A short conversation can often fix small issues before they grow.
3. **Recognize Unhealthy Patterns:** If a friend consistently belittles you or a family member's behavior harms your mental health, it may be time to set firmer limits or seek outside help.
4. **Practice Forgiveness:** Holding onto anger or grudges can create emotional burdens. Sometimes, letting go (when safe and appropriate) frees you to focus on your own growth.

Why It Matters: Good relationships can be a source of support, but troubled ones can drain your mental energy. Keeping them balanced is part of caring for your long-term emotional wellness.

16. Your Strengths

Reminding yourself of what you do well can stabilize your self-esteem. Depression often magnifies flaws and ignores abilities. Taking note of your strengths, whether they are personal qualities or learned skills, can help you remain confident over the long run.

1. **Keep a "Proud Moments" List:** Jot down times when you felt proud—finishing a tough assignment, helping a friend, solving a difficult puzzle.
2. **Ask Trusted People:** If you cannot see your strengths clearly, ask a supportive friend or relative, "What do you think I'm good at?"
3. **Focus on Growth Areas:** Strength is not only about being naturally gifted. It can also be about consistent effort—like improving in math over the semester.
4. **Incorporate Strengths into Daily Life:** If you have a knack for organizing, volunteer to help a friend tidy their locker. If you are good at listening, you might check on someone who seems down.

Why It Matters: Remembering what you do well reinforces the idea that you have value beyond any sadness you might still experience.

---

17. Keeping Perspective About the Future

Teens often face pressure about the future: college decisions, job paths, or uncertain global issues. This can feed anxiety or depression if it feels like everything must be perfect. Finding ways to hold a balanced view of your future can protect your mental health.

1. **Short-Term Focus:** Yes, think about tomorrow or next week—what tasks or goals are relevant? That is easier than planning your entire adult life all at once.
2. **Allow Flexibility:** Your interests might change, and that is okay. Today's plan to study biology might shift to art in a year. You are allowed to evolve.
3. **Seek Guidance:** Talk to school counselors about possible routes. If college is an option, gather information calmly, without panic. If you prefer vocational training or other paths, explore those, too.

4. **Recall You Are Not Alone:** Many teens are uncertain about their future. Even adults do not have it all figured out. It is normal to adjust as you grow.

Why It Matters: Worrying too far ahead can sap your energy in the present. A measured approach to future planning helps you stay focused on maintaining well-being now.

---

18. Handling Success and Positive Changes

You might wonder: if you become happier or do well in school, how do you avoid self-sabotage or fear of losing that progress? Some teens feel strange when good things happen, almost waiting for them to disappear. This can lead to stress or cynicism.

1. **Acknowledge Growth:** It is okay to feel uneasy about improvements, but let yourself see that better days or achievements are real. You worked for them.
2. **Stay Grounded:** Continue the habits that helped you get there—good sleep, healthy social connections—so the improvements have a solid base.
3. **Address Fears:** If you worry you will lose everything, talk it out with a friend, counselor, or family member. They may remind you that gains do not vanish overnight if you stay mindful.
4. **Allow Self-Kindness:** Accepting positive outcomes can sometimes be as hard as handling failure. Remind yourself that you deserve moments of peace or success just as much as anyone else.

Why It Matters: Embracing positive changes without letting anxiety spoil them is part of long-term emotional steadiness.

---

19. Reflecting on Inner Dialogue Over Time

As you maintain well-being, your inner dialogue might have grown kinder. Still, negative thoughts can creep in. Keep an eye on how you talk to yourself, especially during new challenges.

1. **Compare Past and Present Self-Talk:** Maybe before, you harshly blamed yourself for mistakes. Now, you might be more understanding.
2. **Correct New Negative Spirals:** If fresh self-critical voices appear, apply the same techniques you learned—challenge distortions, bring in more balanced thoughts.
3. **Use Evidence:** If you tell yourself, "I'll never pass this exam," recall a similar exam you passed before, or consider that you are studying more effectively now.

Why It Matters: Monitoring self-talk ensures you do not slip back into destructive thought patterns. It keeps your internal environment healthier.

---

20. Encouraging Ongoing Growth and Adaptation

Long-term well-being is not a static achievement. It is about continuous learning, adjusting, and staying open to new methods or experiences. As you move through different life stages—changing schools, entering a new career path, building new friendships—your mental health strategies might evolve, too.

1. **Stay Curious:** If a new hobby, therapy approach, or philosophy resonates, explore it.
2. **Remain Open to Periodic Big Changes:** Maybe you move to a different city or country, or adopt a new perspective on life. Your mental health plan might need updating accordingly.
3. **Use Setbacks as Learning Points:** When you face heartbreak or a job rejection in the future, return to the coping methods that helped you before and consider if new ones are needed.
4. **Encourage Others:** Sharing your experiences with mental health can help friends or younger peers who struggle. Teaching or guiding someone else can strengthen your own resilience.

Why It Matters: Viewing mental wellness as a living, flexible process allows you to stay proactive. You become less likely to be thrown off course by life's unpredictability, since you anticipate and adapt to change.

Chapter 20: Moving Forward and Staying Steady

You have read about recognizing depression, managing everyday challenges, connecting with others, setting goals, and finding supportive strategies that help lift you from intense sadness or hopelessness. At this point, you might wonder what happens next. How do you bring all these ideas into the future and move forward in a more stable way? This concluding chapter will focus on tying it all together—integrating the lessons you have gathered and stepping ahead with a mindset that respects both your progress and the reality that tough days can still come. By reflecting on your strengths, acknowledging potential pitfalls, and staying open to growth, you can craft a path that supports your emotional health over the long haul.

1. Recapping the Tools You Have Discovered

Throughout this book, we have touched on many approaches. It is useful to note which ones resonated with you most. Nobody uses every single strategy equally, and that is normal. By listing your favorites, you can create a personal map of self-help resources.

1. **Emotional Awareness Techniques:** This might include journaling, labeling your emotions, or mindful check-ins.
2. **Coping Skills:** Such as breathing exercises, short walks, listening to music, or reaching out to friends.
3. **Healthy Routines and Habits:** Regular sleep schedules, balanced eating, moderate movement, and planned "device off" times.
4. **Social Support:** Positive peers, family connections, or involvement in clubs that remind you of your worth.
5. **Professional Guidance (If Applicable):** Therapy, counseling, or doctor's visits that have provided structure and accountability.

Why It Matters: Identifying which methods truly help you means you can rely on them when future stressors arise.

2. Finding Your "North Star"

A "North Star" can be a metaphor for something that guides you—an inner sense of direction or a major personal value. It is not necessarily a rigid life goal but something that keeps you anchored when doubts or anxieties appear.

1. **Values Reflection:** Maybe you deeply value compassion, creativity, or fairness. Holding onto these values can shape your choices, giving you purpose.
2. **Personal Mission Statement:** Some teens write a simple statement like, "I want to be kind to others and to myself." This statement can be pinned on a wall or kept in a private journal.
3. **Balanced Ambition:** If you have career or academic goals, tie them to personal meaning. For example, if you care about animals, you might dream of working in veterinary settings or volunteering at a shelter.
4. **Allow It to Evolve:** Your sense of purpose can shift as you gain experiences. Remain open to change if you discover new passions.

Why It Matters: Having a guiding principle helps when you feel lost or discouraged, reminding you that your life can have meaning beyond any immediate struggle.

---

3. Keeping Communication Channels Open

As you move forward, do not forget the importance of honest conversations with people who care about you. Bottling up feelings can make them grow stronger, while sharing them—even briefly—can relieve tension.

1. **Talk to Friends:** If you feel a day is overwhelming, send a message or invite a friend for a quick conversation. Even acknowledging stress out loud can reduce its grip.
2. **Maintain Family or Mentor Relationships:** If certain adults have been supportive, keep them in the loop about your feelings or accomplishments. Positive updates are nice to share too, not just problems.
3. **Counselors and Healthcare Providers:** If you are on medication or in therapy, continue attending sessions as recommended. You can always revisit therapy in the future if you pause it at some point.

4. **Online Forums (with Caution):** In supportive, moderated spaces, you can find encouragement. But be mindful of negative or toxic environments.

Why It Matters: Consistent communication ensures that if warning signs reappear, you have a safety net of people who can help you address them early.

4. Learning to Cope with Change and Uncertainty

Life after high school or as you approach later teen years may involve major changes: transitions to college, job training, family moves, or shifting relationships. Handling these uncertainties can challenge your mental equilibrium. But it can also be a chance for personal development.

1. **View Change as an Opportunity:** Even if it is scary, new environments can bring fresh friends, interesting courses, or better job prospects.
2. **Rely on Portable Coping Skills:** Take your journaling, mindful breathing, or short daily goals with you wherever you go. They do not depend on location.
3. **Stay Flexible:** If one path does not work out (e.g., you do not get into your top college choice), remember other routes exist. This resilience can reduce panic when plans shift.
4. **Create Familiar Comforts in New Spaces:** If you move to a dorm or a new home, set up a cozy corner with items that calm you—photos, a blanket, a small plant.

Why It Matters: Being ready for change, instead of avoiding it, lowers stress and keeps depression from having an easy inroad during big life transitions.

5. Strengthening Self-Compassion

The concept of self-compassion means treating yourself with understanding and support rather than constant self-criticism. This can be a lifelong practice, but it plays a big role in maintaining emotional balance.

1. **Recognize Inner Kindness:** Notice if you talk to yourself harshly. Ask, "Would I say this to a friend?" If not, try rephrasing it gently.

2. **Acknowledge Setbacks Without Harsh Blame:** If you slip into old habits—like negative self-talk or skipping self-care—remind yourself that everyone stumbles. What matters is getting back on track.
3. **Practice Physical Self-Soothing:** Sometimes hugging a pillow, petting a cat, or placing a hand on your chest can bring a sense of comfort during stressful moments.

Why It Matters: Compassion toward yourself can reduce shame, which often fuels depression. It also helps you bounce back faster from mistakes.

6. Balancing Realism and Hope

Teen years can be full of drama—some of it can feel deeply negative. Staying upbeat while acknowledging reality can be tricky. You do not want to be oblivious to real issues, but you also do not want to give in to complete despair.

1. **Realistic Outlook:** Accept difficulties as part of life. A conflict with a friend or a tough exam is not proof you are doomed, but it might be a signal to apply problem-solving or coping skills.
2. **Hope as a Choice:** Even if you are uncertain, you can decide to hold a bit of hope that things can improve or at least that you can handle challenges better.
3. **Create Solution-Oriented Thoughts:** If a problem arises, focus on "What can I do next?" rather than "It's all ruined." Even small steps matter.
4. **Avoid Catastrophic Language:** Phrases like "I'll never recover" or "Everything is over" can intensify sadness. Replace them with more measured words like "This is hard, but I can seek help."

Why It Matters: Balancing realism and hope prevents you from getting stuck in toxic positivity or in an all-negative mindset. It allows you to navigate life with a sense of capability and possibility.

7. Maintaining Boundaries to Protect Your Well-Being

Long-term steadiness includes safeguarding yourself from environments or relationships that consistently drain or harm you. Boundaries help you choose when and how you engage with potentially stressful people or situations.

1. **Peer Pressure Management:** If friends push you toward behaviors that feel unsafe or hurtful, practice saying, "No, I'm not comfortable with that."
2. **Social Media Boundaries:** Unfollow or mute accounts that cause emotional distress. Block negativity if needed.
3. **Family Boundaries:** Even with relatives, it is okay to state that you need personal space or prefer certain topics not to be discussed if they only lead to arguments.
4. **Time Boundaries:** If constant messages from someone overwhelm you, let them know you cannot be available 24/7. Set times you are open to chat or respond.

Why It Matters: Boundaries do not make you selfish. They protect your emotional stability so you can maintain the progress you have worked hard for.

---

8. Revisiting Professional Options Over Time

As you grow older, new or different professional resources may become available. You might discover therapy styles that did not exist when you were younger, or you might qualify for certain groups or scholarship-based programs aimed at supporting mental health.

1. **Specialized Therapies:** If you initially had talk therapy, later you might try art therapy, music therapy, or a certain evidence-based approach like CBT (Cognitive Behavioral Therapy) or DBT (Dialectical Behavior Therapy).
2. **Support Groups for Specific Interests:** Some groups focus on teen anxiety, LGBTQ+ support, grief processing, or other specific concerns you might relate to.
3. **Medication Adjustments:** If you take medication, a new stage of life might require dose changes, different prescriptions, or new combinations. This should be managed with a doctor's advice.
4. **Transitions from Pediatric to Adult Care:** Around 18 or older, you might shift from a pediatric mental health provider to adult services. Plan this transition so you do not lose continuity of care.

Why It Matters: Ongoing mental health care can adapt to your changing needs. Staying informed and open-minded keeps your support network aligned with who you are becoming.

9. Encouraging Others While Protecting Yourself

Having traveled a path of managing depression, you might feel empathy for others going through similar pain. You might want to lend a listening ear or share tips. While supporting friends is kind, maintain a boundary so you do not absorb more stress than you can handle.

1. **Offer Empathy, Not Rescue:** It is great to say, "I'm here to listen," but remember you cannot singlehandedly fix someone else's deep issues.
2. **Recommend Professional Help:** If a friend seems in crisis or talks about self-harm, encourage them to seek a counselor or hotline. Offer to go with them if it feels right, but do not try to replace expert aid.
3. **Watch for Compassion Fatigue:** If you become overwhelmed by others' problems, step back. It is okay to politely say, "I'm feeling overloaded right now."

Why It Matters: Supporting others can reinforce your own progress, but not if it drains you to a point of relapse. Balanced compassion ensures you stay well, too.

---

10. Handling Setbacks in a Mature Way

Even with the best plans, you might face a tough day, a heartbreak, or an anxiety spike. How you respond can shape whether you bounce back or sink deeper.

1. **Pause and Assess:** Instead of panicking, remind yourself, "I've been through difficult moments before and found ways to cope."
2. **Use Your Toolkit:** Return to the specific strategies you trust—like journaling, short walks, or contacting someone who understands.
3. **Review the Situation Objectively:** If something went wrong—like failing a test—evaluate what actually happened. Did you not study enough? Were there external factors? Then decide on a plan to improve or seek help.
4. **Be Willing to Ask for Extra Support:** A serious setback may call for scheduling a therapy appointment or having a longer talk with a trusted adult.

Why It Matters: Setbacks are part of life. Handling them calmly and methodically can prevent a small drop in mood from spiraling into a full-blown crisis.

11. Acknowledging How Far You Have Come

Reflecting on your past experiences with depression can highlight the growth you have achieved. Even if you still have low moods sometimes, you likely have gained awareness, resilience, or better coping skills. Recognizing this helps reinforce your confidence in dealing with future challenges.

1. **Compare Then and Now:** Think back to a time when your depression was at its worst. What improvements do you see in how you handle stress today?
2. **Note the Skills You Gained:** Perhaps you are more comfortable speaking up about feelings, or you have discovered creative outlets for sadness.
3. **Remember the People Who Supported You:** Mentally thank them (or do it out loud if you wish). Knowing others stood by you can strengthen your sense of connectedness.
4. **Use This Perspective:** Remind yourself that if you could make progress before, you can do it again whenever you face obstacles.

Why It Matters: Depression often tries to convince you that you are still stuck. Looking back with clarity reveals that you have made headway, even if it was gradual.

---

12. Embracing Lifelong Learning About Yourself

Self-discovery does not end after teenage years. You will keep learning new things about your personality, preferences, triggers, and sources of joy. Maintaining emotional well-being is easier when you treat each phase of life as an ongoing exploration.

1. **Try Different Experiences:** Sign up for a new class or visit new places if possible. Each experience can teach you something about your tastes and resilience.
2. **Reflect After Events:** Did volunteering at a local fair energize you or drain you? Understanding these reactions helps guide future decisions.
3. **Adapt Old Skills to New Contexts:** Mindfulness might look different in college than in high school, or your friend group might shift. Evolve your methods accordingly.

4. **Stay Flexible in Identity:** People sometimes cling to labels about who they are—"I'm always shy," or "I'm a perfectionist." Allow room for those traits to shift over time as you grow.

Why It Matters: Recognizing that you are a dynamic individual helps you handle new phases or challenges without feeling locked into old patterns.

---

13. Creating a Personal Maintenance Plan

Consider writing a concise "maintenance plan" that outlines your main self-care practices, warning signs, and response steps. It can be one page or saved on your phone. This is your quick reference guide to staying steady.

1. **Daily Essentials:** Note the minimum self-care you want daily—like eight hours of sleep, one healthy meal, or a brief relaxation exercise.
2. **Weekly Checkpoints:** Could include a short "how am I feeling?" journal entry or a social outing with a friend.
3. **Warning Signs Section:** List behaviors (like skipping meals or ignoring messages) that signal a possible slide. Next to each, note a coping response.
4. **Emergency Contacts:** Write down the phone numbers of a trusted adult, a friend, a mental health hotline, or your counselor. Keep them easily accessible.

Why It Matters: In low moments, you might forget your coping skills or feel too drained to think. Having a maintenance plan on hand can guide you step by step.

---

14. Using Visual or Physical Reminders of Progress

Some teens find it helpful to keep a small token or symbol of their resilience. It could be a bracelet, a keychain, or a piece of art. Whenever they see it, they recall that they have fought hard against depression and continue to stand.

1. **Craft a Personalized Item:** For instance, paint a small rock with an inspiring word or phrase. Keep it on your desk.

2. **Collect Affirmation Notes:** Write short positive messages from friends or compliments you have received. Store them in a jar and read them when feeling low.
3. **Choose a Symbol That Speaks to You:** It could be a phoenix if you resonate with rising from ashes, a leaf symbolizing growth, or any object that represents hope.
4. **Focus on the Meaning:** The item is not magic; it is a prompt reminding you of your inner strength and the support you have.

Why It Matters: Such tokens can break through negative thought spirals, offering a concrete reminder of your progress and capability for endurance.

---

15. Celebrating Milestones Gently

While depression might still visit occasionally, there will be times you notice real strides: feeling calmer in stressful situations, receiving positive feedback from a teacher or boss, or going several weeks without intense sadness. Recognizing these moments can maintain your motivation.

1. **Small Acknowledgments:** Treat yourself to a favorite snack, spend an afternoon reading for fun, or watch a movie you have been meaning to see.
2. **Share with Someone:** Let a friend or family member know, "I handled a tough day better than before," or "I turned in all my assignments on time." It feels good to be heard.
3. **Mindful Reflection:** Jot down what helped you achieve that milestone. Keep it in mind for future challenges.
4. **Plan Ongoing Goals:** Use the momentum to set a new, slightly bigger goal—maybe improving your exercise routine or exploring a new hobby.

Why It Matters: Giving yourself credit cements your efforts as worthwhile. It counters the negative voice that says nothing changes or that you do not deserve positive feedback.

16. Accepting the Normalcy of Emotional Ups and Downs

A stable emotional life does not mean you never feel sadness or frustration again. It means you handle these feelings in healthier ways and do not remain stuck. A realistic view of well-being allows for normal human emotions without labeling every low day as a crisis.

1. **Embrace Ordinary Mood Swings:** Some days might just be "meh," and that is okay. You do not have to fix every dip instantly.
2. **Distinguish Between a Dip and a Major Relapse:** If you are tired for an afternoon, that might be normal. If you find yourself withdrawing entirely and feeling hopeless daily, that might be a sign to act.
3. **Self-Validate Both Good and Bad Moments:** Affirm that it is normal to feel happy sometimes and to feel sad sometimes. Neither is "wrong."
4. **Stay Compassionate:** If negative feelings last or intensify, be gentle with yourself and refer back to your coping plan or talk to someone.

Why It Matters: Viewing emotional fluctuations as part of life eases the pressure to be in a perfect mood all the time. This perspective reduces self-blame and fosters acceptance.

---

17. Remaining Open to Gradual Growth

Even if you have largely overcome a depressive episode, further development and healing can continue for months or years. That might involve learning deeper stress-management methods, refining relationship skills, or discovering new passions.

1. **Avoid the "I'm Done" Mindset:** Thinking you are done forever with self-improvement can leave you unprepared for future stress.
2. **Embrace Lifelong Adjustment:** As you face adult challenges—jobs, relationships, independence—your mental tools may need updates.
3. **Stay Curious About Therapy or Self-Help:** If you read a new book on mental health and find a fresh technique, try it. Growth is ongoing.

Why It Matters: The idea that personal growth keeps going stops you from feeling shocked when you encounter new emotional challenges. You expect to keep evolving and can meet obstacles with a calmer mindset.

18. Balancing Independence with Seeking Assistance

As you become more confident, you might want to do everything on your own. While independence is great, do not cut off help entirely. Checking in with others or occasionally returning to therapy for a tune-up can keep you from slipping unnoticed into older patterns.

1. **Identify Areas You Manage Well:** Maybe you handle everyday stress okay now, so you no longer need weekly counselor visits.
2. **Identify Areas That May Require Guidance:** If you struggle with bigger transitions or severe triggers, keep a plan for when to bring others in.
3. **Stay Honest with Trusted Individuals:** If you pretend you are fine to preserve independence, you might miss timely assistance.
4. **Offer Mutual Support:** Friendships thrive on balanced give-and-take. Accepting help does not mean losing self-sufficiency; it is part of being human.

Why It Matters: Striving for total isolation can backfire, especially if a serious problem arises. A moderate approach ensures a healthy mix of independence and community.

---

19. Reflecting on Self-Worth Outside Achievements

As a teen, achievements—grades, sports success, or social popularity—might seem central to your identity. But overemphasizing them can strain your mental health. Long-term stability often involves seeing your self-worth as more than external success.

1. **Notice Personal Traits Beyond Performance:** Are you a caring friend, a creative thinker, or someone who shows empathy? These qualities matter just as much as awards.
2. **Diversify Your Identity:** Explore different hobbies or volunteer in new areas to learn about who you are beyond any single role.
3. **Handle Failures More Kindly:** If a project fails, remember that does not define your entire being. You still retain your personality, compassion, and growth potential.

4. **Seek Genuine Fulfillment:** Instead of chasing achievements for approval, look for pursuits you genuinely enjoy or find meaningful.

Why It Matters: Grounding self-worth in multiple aspects of your identity can protect you from a spiral if one area falls short.

---

20. Moving Forward with Confidence and Realism

By weaving together self-compassion, healthy habits, supportive relationships, and a willingness to keep learning, you lay a foundation for navigating future seasons of life. There will be moments of stress or sorrow, but they do not have to trap you in despair. You have tools now—emotional awareness, practical coping methods, and hopefully a network of trusted people—and you can keep building on these. Rather than a perfect end point, this stage is an open door to further exploration, personal growth, and meaningful connections.

1. **Set Ongoing Intentions:** Maybe you aim to maintain a balanced schedule, remain open to therapy if needed, and periodically re-evaluate your emotional state.
2. **Embrace the Possibility of Good Days:** Let yourself enjoy times when you feel lighter, or when an achievement feels earned. You are allowed to feel content without guilt.
3. **Stay Brave in the Face of Challenges:** Courage is not the absence of fear, but the decision to act despite it. With depression or anxiety, that might mean continuing your daily tasks even when negative thoughts appear.
4. **Keep Others in Mind:** Sometimes, focusing on being kind or supportive to others can remind you of your strengths and community ties.

Why It Matters: Forward momentum in life is built on daily choices. By leaning on the progress you have made and staying flexible about the future, you stand a better chance of remaining steady, whatever arises.

Final Thoughts

Depression does not define you. It is one aspect of your story, shaped by multiple factors—biology, environment, personal history—but not the whole of who you are or where you are headed. The chapters in this book aimed to offer insights into recognizing signs of depression, reaching out for help, and building coping habits that support your emotional health. By practicing these ideas and adapting them to your life, you can keep depression from holding you back.

Remember, if you ever feel yourself sliding into deep hopelessness or self-harm thoughts, that is your cue to reconnect with a counselor, a loved one, or professional care right away. Seeking help is a sign of self-respect, not weakness. You deserve continued support, understanding, and the chance to enjoy life's moments of peace or excitement.

Moving forward is not about racing ahead to a flawless existence. It is about taking each day as it arrives—using learned strategies, staying open to growth, and forgiving yourself when you stumble. Over time, these everyday choices accumulate into a life that feels more stable, purposeful, and true to who you are. Even if depression lingers on the margins or occasionally flares up, you now have the tools to face it and keep going. You can nurture a future that balances challenges with the possibility of hope, connection, and personal fulfillment. And that, in the end, is a powerful form of strength.

www.ingramcontent.com/pod-product-compliance
Lightning Source LLC
LaVergne TN
LVHW012044070526
838202LV00056B/5591